7511930

-C. JUL 979

RUSSELL, V.
3.95

NEW FOREST
PONIES

636.16

06. 05. 94 COUNTY

R SER C STOCK

OKSTORE

ELEX 1512

3 NOV 197

26. OC 1989

-7 AUG 1982

24. JUL. 1982

1 5 APR 1994

9 MAM 1994

4 FEB 1997

1 2 FEB 1997

5 MARCH

18 AUG 1999

13 JUL 2000

L 33

D1626501

NEW FOREST PONIES

New Forest Ponies

Valerie Russell

DAVID & CHARLES

NEWTON ABBOT LONDON

NORTH POMFRET(VT) VANCOUVER

To my mother

ISBN 0 7153 7162 2
Library of Congress Catalog Card Number 76-8627

Set in 11 on 13pt Garamond
and printed in Great Britain
by Latimer Trend & Company Ltd Plymouth
for David & Charles (Publishers) Limited
Brunel House Newton Abbot Devon

Published in the United States of America
by David & Charles Inc
North Pomfret Vermont 05053 USA

Published in Canada
by Douglas David & Charles Limited
1875 Welch Street North Vancouver BC

CONTENTS

LIST OF ILLUSTRATIONS

THE IDEAL PONY

New Forest ponies can claim, with justification, to be the most versatile of the mountain and moorland breeds and the ones that best fit the description 'genuine family ponies'. There are few equestrian activities in which they have not competed with distinction – show-jumping, hunting, long-distance riding, polo, pony-racing, dressage, driving, or eventing – and it is by no means unheard of for the same pony to take an enthusiastic part in all these sports, the several members of the family, from parents down to the youngest child, riding him in different events. Since the end of World War II the popularity of the ponies has increased dramatically, as more and more families have come to realise that the breed combines speed and handiness with extraordinary weight-carrying capabilities, in addition to being tremendous fun to own and ride.

THE FORESTER

There are a number of reasons for the ponies' remarkable adaptability, and their actual 'make and shape' provide at least some of them. The New Forest pony is regarded as one of the large native breeds, with a maximum height of 14·2 hands, and although there is no official minimum, few are under 12 hands.

For descriptive purposes they are divided into Type A ponies, which range from 13·1 to 14·2 hands, and are well up to an adult's weight, yet narrow enough for children, and type B, which are up to 13·1. Colour may be anything except piebald and skewbald, but bay is the most common.

Although less distinctive in appearance than some other mountain and moorland breeds, a good Forester possesses all the qualities of an attractive riding pony, with plenty of bone and depth of body, strong quarters, long clean sloping shoulders, straight limbs, well sloped pasterns, hard round feet, and a well-set head. Many stud-owners all over Britain and abroad aim at this ideal, and there are plenty of ponies, both in and out of the show-ring, which come very close to it.

The average pony, however, including some bred on the Forest under much less controlled conditions than are possible on studs, often presents a slightly different picture. While nearly always having excellent shoulders, limbs and feet, some may have less desirable features, such as a rather large head (although this may be balanced by a relatively short neck), a longish back, drooping quarters, and a low set tail. These faults rarely affect the ponies' performance, however, and what they may lack in sheer show-ring beauty they more than make up for by their other qualities of character and temperament. For showing purposes a certain amount of judicious trimming can do wonders to make the head look smaller, while in classes where mane-plaiting is appropriate a greater number of smaller plaits than usual helps to give the appearance of a longer neck. The natural good sloping shoulder can be emphasised by a straight-cut saddle.

One of the outstanding physical characteristics of the ponies, and arguably the one contributing most to their adaptability, is their excellent action. This is almost invariably free and straight, coming from the top of the shoulder and not from the elbow – an attribute that, together with their sure-footedness, has probably developed over the centuries through the necessity to 'use themselves' fully in order to travel swiftly and safely over the rugged terrain of their homeland. Although the paces of the average Forester lack the extravagance, for example, of the Welsh ponies, the facts that they use their shoulders freely, usually have good pasterns and bring their hocks well under them, are of paramount importance in the various activities in which they take part. In endurance riding, for instance, when an animal must keep going at a steady even pace for hour after hour, broken by short bursts at the canter, the Foresters' longstriding walk and easy level trot are ideal, and their rhythmic canter and ground-covering gallop enable them to keep up a good average speed with a minimum of effort. In faster sports, such as polo, show-jumping and gymkhanas, where manoeuvrability is at a premium, and it is essential for a pony to have its hocks well under it, the Foresters again do well. They are also exceptionally fast for their size.

Of all their paces, the canter is probably the best, almost certainly because it is more natural to them than the trot or the gallop. Those bred on the Forest are disturbed from time to time, by the annual round-ups, by hunts, and sometimes by dogs, and it is noticeable that they frequently move straight from a walk into a canter, which is the least tiring pace for moving through the thick-growing heather of the open moorland. Thus it is comparatively rare to see New Forest ponies involved in that sad picture of the novice show-ring – a small child trying desperately to induce a canter in a pony that just trots faster and faster.

Of great importance in a family pony is the 'feel' it gives to its riders particularly to the adults, who perhaps think they may be under-horsed on an animal standing less than 15 hands. In this respect, the larger Forest ponies, with their long free stride, give a comfortable ride with much more of a 'horsey' feel. This is much less tiring for adults accustomed to full-sized horses than the 'proppiness' associated with the smaller (and indeed some of the larger) native breeds. An added advantage is that the Foresters seem to retain their paces and elasticity of movement into old age, probably because of their good shoulders and pasterns.

Good movement and conformation, substance, and a considerable size range all contribute to versatility, but the ability to adapt readily depends to a large extent on temperament, and in this the New Forest ponies are second to none. They show the intelligence, commonsense and courage typical of most mountain and moorland breeds, but in addition they are kindly, generous and exceptionally docile to handle – even the stallions are easily broken in and make completely safe and beautifully mannered mounts for adults and children alike. As a breed, they lack the stubbornness and cunning of some native ponies, and although usually kind and sensible, they are anything but dull. Most owners are constantly surprised and delighted by their pony's ability to think for itself, to extricate itself from difficulties (often not of its own making) and to demonstrate that indefinable but priceless quality 'character'.

As riding ponies, many show a delightful willingness to adapt to the needs and limitations of different riders, as the following story of a well known mare illustrates. Beacon Periwinkle enjoys jumping classes at local shows, and has made it quite clear that she knows exactly what is required of her at the various stages in the competition. In the first rounds, when time is unimportant, she jumps happily round at her own pace, not exerting herself unduly but usually going clear. However, when it comes to the timed jump-off, she pulls out all the stops without any urging from her rider, cuts the corners, and skims over the fences with the will to win apparent in every line of her small body. One day, having just galloped flat-out in the jump-off of the 13·2 and under class, she was immediately put into the class for riders of 11 years and under, carrying a much less experienced and rather insecure jockey. Nine out of ten ponies, under similar circumstances, would have taken off from sheer excitement – but not Periwinkle. She went round the little course steadily and carefully, coming back to a trot between fences, and obviously taking care of her young rider. They qualified for the jump-off, and although she went faster she still took great care, and at one stage, when her jockey landed up round her ears, she threw him back in the saddle with a toss of her head. Similar tales of the kindness and character of the New Forest ponies are legion.

The excellent temperament of the ponies is in many ways due to the Forest itself and the conditions within it. Even today, when there are a number of private studs throughout Britain, the majority of the breed owned by families up and down the country have been born in or very close to the Forest, or have run on it in their early years. The typical amenability of both Forest and stud-bred ponies is surely the result of their descent from countless generations of animals that lived in close proximity to people who walked, rode and drove among them daily. Being handled and broken-in, therefore, is probably a less traumatic experience for them than for mountain and moorland breeds whose native heaths are more remote.

Many herds of ponies live in and around the villages in the New Forest, wandering freely up and down the lanes, and pausing from time to time to test the security of the catch on a garden gate. Some of the clever old mares have a talent for opening all but special anti-pony catches, while others indulge in a peculiarly destructive form of rhythmic pushing against slightly suspect gates or fences, which give in a surprisingly short time. Others simply jump gates, fences or cattle grids, and there can be few local residents who have escaped the devastation caused by hungry ponies in the garden. Once in, their almost contemptuous familiarity with people makes them extremely difficult to dislodge – it is almost as if they know that under Forest law, it is the householder's responsibility to keep them out of his property. Anyone considering buying an animal they know to have been bred on the Forest should ensure that all stable doors and field gates are really pony-proof, and even stud-bred ponies have been known to inherit their ancestors' catch-opening talents.

A vital attribute of a good family pony is complete reliability in traffic. Having been accustomed since birth to the thousands of cars and lorries on the roads criss-crossing their traditional territories, New Forest ponies are not so much traffic-proof as almost totally impervious to it: even the largest Juggernauts thundering past cause no more than a ruffling of their manes and tails.

The average Forester, then, has an excellent temperament, and its make and shape should be such that it is capable of giving a safe comfortable ride to both adults and children. It is difficult to define a distinctive 'type', however. No one with even an elementary knowledge of ponies could mistake a Shetland, a Welsh mountain pony, or an Exmoor, for any other breed, but the Forester has been notorious for not having a true type – or perhaps more accurately for having several types. To understand why this should be, it is necessary to take a brief look at their history.

HISTORY

The origins of the New Forest pony belong to pre-history, but the breed is believed to be indigenous and was almost certainly known to the ancient Britons. In her book *Walking in the New Forest*, Joan Begbie describes them as being descended 'direct from the courageous little beasts who drew the scythe-wheeled war chariots into battle in the days of wolves and woad'. In the days when the moors and forests of southern England stretched practically unbroken from Southampton to Dartmoor, and even possibly to the fringes of Exmoor, herds of wild ponies are believed to have wandered freely over the area. It thus seems reasonable to assume that the southern native breeds of Dartmoor, New Forest, and Exmoor have common ancestors, and it is thought they probably bore a close resemblance to the latter. With the advance of civilisation, sections of the forest and moors were cultivated, so that the ponies were restricted much more to the areas from which the present-day breeds take their names. In such a manner separate development of the breeds may have begun.

Few references to the New Forest ponies are known before the time of Canute, and although they are mentioned in the Domesday Book, it is far from clear if they were wild in the sense of being ownerless, or whether they were turned out by private owners much as they are today. Thus it is not possible to decide if any form of selective breeding took place, although it is known that in 1208 eighteen Welsh mares were introduced, presumably with the idea of improving existing stock. Some official attempts to improve the breed of ponies on unenclosed land were made in the Middle Ages, culminating in the Statute of the Drift of the Forest in 1224, which was intended to ensure that poor specimens brought in on the annual round-up were put down. About 1540 Henry VIII ordered that all (entire) horses under 14 hands (or 14 'handfulls', as it was then termed) were to be slaughtered, but clearly this edict was not carried out, though there is reason to believe that the height of some Forest ponies had increased from 11 or 12 hands to about 13 hands by Elizabethan times. There is, however, no truth in the story that the breed was influenced by Spanish horses that swam ashore from the doomed ships of the Armada, and indeed the story that any of the horses at all landed in Britain is almost certainly apocryphal.

From the scant generalised descriptions available, most Forest ponies before the mid-nineteenth century seemed to have been stocky, rather shaggy animals averaging about 12 hands, and of undistinguished appearance. One early eighteenth-century writer described them as 'the property of vagrants and smugglers not worth more than 2/6 a head'.

The first undisputed record of an attempt to improve the breed by the introduction of outside blood (as distinct from elimination of poor or undersized specimens) dates from 1765, when the thoroughbred stallion Markse, bought at Tattersall's sale of the Duke of Cumberland's horses, was brought down to the district by a Dorsetshire farmer. For the next four years Markse stood at stud, covering Forest mares at a fee of half a guinea. On the influence of Markse, Sir Walter Gilby in his book *Thoroughbred and Other Ponies* comments that 'the New Forest breed of ponies were being improved by the very best TB blood, the effects of which continued to be apparent for many years after Markse had left the district'. The reason for his abrupt departure was the phenomenal success of one of his sons, the legendary Eclipse. Clearly a stallion that could sire an Eclipse was thought too valuable to spend the rest of his life producing cross-bred native ponies. From the point of view of the breed as a whole, however, the lasting influence of Markse is debatable. He never ran on the Forest, and only served selected mares, and it seems likely that the progeny would have been sold away before passing on the influence to the native-bred ponies.

That some form of selective breeding took place in the eighteenth century can be inferred from statements of the Rev William Gilpin, Vicar of Boldre near Lymington, in his book *Remarks on Forest Scenery* (1784). Commenting on the diminutive size of the ponies, he remarked: 'In point of value the New Forest horse would ride higher if the same care was taken in the breeding him as was formerly taken . . .' From the same author we have definite evidence that some quality at least had been bred into a few ponies, although his description of the majority could all too easily fit some of the poorer specimens to be seen today. He says,

I have also heard of a grey mare purchased at the age of 6 years in the neighbourhood of Brockenhurst, wild from the forest . . . She was rather more than 13 hands high; was finely made; had a round body; beautiful head and neck; and limbs like those of a deer. But her motions were still more admirable. Her paces and mouth were uncommonly pleasant and her power of action was surprising.

The plate on p 17 is a lithograph by Gilpin's brother of the 'improved' and the 'ordinary' ponies, and of them the author had this to say:

> The grey horse represented in the annexed plate is among the most beautiful. But it general the croup of the forest-horse is low and his head ill-set-on having what the jockies call a *stiff-jaw*. Of this defect a resemblance is given in the horse on the left, whose head is set on as those of the New Forest horses commonly are. Their claim, therefore, to high lineage, must in general rest more on their good qualities than on their beauty – on the hardiness of their character – on their uncommon strength – on their agility and sureness of foot, which they probably acquire by constantly lifting their legs among the furze.

The grey was evidently one of the few high-class ponies to be found on the Forest in the second half of the eighteenth century. Little improvement occurred during the next 50 or so years, as is evidenced by James Duncan's description in the *Quarterly Journal of Agriculture* of 1840:

> The most remarkable of their peculiarities consists in the length of the back, which is considerably depressed or curved downwards; it is probably owing to the formation of the spine, in connection with the circumstance of their food always consisting of grass, that the belly is unusually large and prominent, appearing as if the animals were with foal. The head is large and somewhat clumsy; according to Gilpin it is ill set on . . . Although clean and tolerably handsome, the legs are too short in proportion to the length of the body . . .

By the middle of the nineteenth century, therefore, the New Forest pony had moved some distance from the generally accepted primitive type, but just how this came about is still conjectural. Inbreeding must have played a part, together with the indefinable

influence of environment, which inevitably contributes significantly to the development of any breed. The New Forest pony
had become more or less of a type, though a less than beautiful
one, by this time.

Little more is heard of efforts to improve the breed until the
mid-nineteenth century, but it seems certain that Arabs were used
at various times, as a distinct 'Eastern type' has been noted by
writers from the late nineteenth century up to the present day.
Organised attempts at improvement may be said to have begun in
1852, when the Prince Consort offered Queen Victoria's Arab
stallion Zorah to stand at New Park. Until quite recently the
influence of this horse on the breed has been regarded as considerable but an examination of facts newly unearthed, points in
the other direction. Standing at New Park, the stallion never ran
out on the Forest and covered only selected mares. For various
reasons the scheme was not a success and Zorah left after four
years, during which time he covered only 112 mares. It seems unlikely, therefore, that he made anything but a marginal impression
on the breed. Efforts at improvement continued, and in 1885
officials of the Forest hired four well-bred stallions to be used on the
Commoners' mares, and in 1889 the Queen sent two further Arab
stallions – Abagan (a gift from the Iman of Muscat) and Yuresson.
The chief aim of the improvers was to introduce some quality
into Forest ponies, and particularly to increase their size. At
various times not only Arab and TB blood were used, but carthorse and hackney blood as well. The last two did nothing to
improve the quality, and while all four out-crosses tended to increase size, this in itself led to a decrease in bone, substance, and
the all-important hardiness essential for ponies in face of the
rigours of Forest life.

Then, in the closing years of the last century, that great authority
on pony-breeding, Lord Arthur Cecil, noted the lack of bone and
substance in the average Forester and decided to do something
about it. He believed that the best way to eradicate the faults he
saw was to breed from native ponies of a sturdier type, and in
1893 began the importation of stallions that were to have a
profound influence on the subsequent development of the breed.

The first 'foreigners' came from Rhum, to be followed by Fells, Dales, more Highlands, Dartmoors, and Exmoors, (including some of Sir Frederick Knight's) and later Lord Lucas imported Welsh stallions of the famous Dyoll Starlight strain. In the first decade of this century a pony stallion was officially accepted as a sire of a New Forest pony provided it stood within the New Forest Parliamentary district, irrespective of its breed. It might be thought that this massive influx of outside blood would destroy for all time any semblance of a distinctive New Forest pony, particularly as it continued until the 1930s; but as Lord Arthur Cecil himself remarked, 'owing to the mysterious power of nature to grind down and assimilate all these types to the one most suited to the land', a more or less distinctive type began to emerge in due course. With the ban on further infusions of outside blood in the 1930s, the type showed definite signs of becoming 'fixed', though certain characteristics of other native breeds could still be detected in the ponies running on the Forest.

Fascinating confirmation of the ponies' reversion to type is given in T. F. Dale's introduction to the first *Stud Book* in 1910. He discusses a portrait of a Forest pony of 1814, which:

> ... has all the characteristic defects and excellencies we are accustomed to look for in the Forest ponies of the present day. She has a fairly large, but remarkably Eastern type of head, a rather short neck, a long back, drooping and rather narrow quarters. She is high on the hock, light-boned beneath the knee and hock, but a good shoulder and great depth through the heart.

Today, over 160 years and countless out-crosses later, ponies answering that general description can still be seen on the Forest. In recent years, however, with the increase in ponies bred on private studs and holdings, the breed is tending to diversify again. With so much outside blood but a few generations back, selective breeding allows the perpetuation of, for example, the Arab type, the Welsh type, or even the 'horsey' type. Thus, of all our mountain and moorland ponies, the Forester is by far the most mixed in recent ancestry, and the difficulties of defining a type in the same way as can be done for, say, a Welsh pony are all too apparent.

Plate 1 Ideal type (in foreground) and 'common' specimen of Forest pony about 1790

Plate 2 The Agisters of 1910: Jesse Taylor (right), Charles Evemy (centre), and his son Albert (left)

Plate 3 Agister Raymond Bennett tail-marking a pony

Plate 4 Forest mare showing protective moustache

2

ADMINISTRATORS, COMMONERS
AND OTHERS

The various attempts at improving the breed have left their mark, but the greatest influence has always been the New Forest itself and the conditions prevailing within it. Over the centuries the ponies have developed a unique way of life in adapting to their environment, which presents a variety of habitats, nearly all of which they have learned to use to their advantage.

VERDERERS AND AGISTERS

Although the ponies wander free and unrestricted, they are not wild in the true sense of not belonging to anyone. They belong to the commoners – the occupiers of land that carries 'Right of Common of Pasture'. This ancient right dates back at least to Norman times, when the whole area was subject to the very severe Forest law, drawn up in order to preserve deer for royal hunting. Under the law owners of land within the designated boundaries were forbidden to fence their property, as this would interfere with the freedom of the deer. They were allowed to turn their stock out for limited periods only. From November 22 to 4 May (the Winter Heyning) natural feed was scarce and domestic animals could not be allowed to compete for it with the deer; and from 20 June to 20 July (the Fence Month) the deer were dropping their young, and it was essential that they should be left undisturbed. During these months, which amounted to more than half the year, commonable stock had to be kept on the owners' land, either in byres or tethered, and it was not until the New Forest Act of 1877 that the right to turn out (depasture) stock, including ponies, all the year round was granted.

Although all the ponies are privately owned, the responsibility for their welfare and for looking after the commoners' rights, rests with a body of five appointed and five elected representatives with a wide knowledge of the Forest and its stock, who together make up the Court of Verderers. The elected verderers, who must be commoners occupying at least an acre of land bearing Right of Pasture, are elected by fellow-commoners who must also occupy a minimum of an acre. The remaining five are the Official Verderer appointed by the Crown, and one each by the Ministry of Agriculture, the Forestry Commission, the Countryside Commission, and the Planning Authority. As a body they are responsible not only for the physical well-being of the commonable animals (they have the power to order the removal from the Forest of any animal if they consider it is being caused to suffer) and for approving all stallions to be turned out, but they must also consider a welter of proposals for the recreational use of the area – plans for roads, drainage schemes and so on. The verderers also work in close consultation with the Forestry Commission.

In addition to their administrative duties, the verderers sit as a court in the Verderers Hall at the Queen's House, Lyndhurst, on at least six Mondays each year. To this court may come anyone with a suggestion or complaint about matters of local (Forest) significance. This is called 'making a presentment', and an answer will be given, sometimes at the next meeting. Certain of the verderers also sit in a judicial capacity as the Court of Swainmote, to try offences committed against its own or the Forestry Commission's bylaws – for example, it is an offence to turn out a stallion that has not been passed to run on the Forest.

The verderers also maintain close links with the New Forest Pony Breeding and Cattle Society, and indeed the present secretary of the society, Miss Dionis Macnair, is a verderer. Pony society judges often assist with the inspection and passing of stallions to run out, and the two bodies cooperate fully in efforts to improve the standard of Forest-bred animals.

Area 1.

Area 2.

Area 3.

Diagrams showing pattern of tail-markings used to identify the district in which a pony has been turned out, and
as a sign that the marking fee has been paid.

Though ultimately responsible for the welfare of the ponies, the
verderers appoint three full-time officers, known as agisters, to
carry out the practical supervision necessary. The duties of these
agisters include patrolling their districts, looking into accidents to
commoners' animals, and ordering the removal of sick, injured, or
poor stock from the Forest when necessary.

COMMONERS AND OTHER BODIES

Inevitably the commoners, who, understandably if incorrectly, regard the New Forest as their own special preserve, sometimes come into conflict with other bodies who have a particular interest in the area. Their views are made known through the Commoners' Defence Association, which was founded about the turn of the century to safeguard their rights and interests. Riders, walkers, motorists, campers, and, perhaps most significantly, naturalists and conservationists, all have legitimate claims on this beautiful part of the country. While acknowledging the rights of the public, the commoners regard the recreational use of the Forest as a considerable threat. Until the recent introduction of Car-free Zones, with the accompanying physical barriers to prevent motorists driving anywhere they could within the perambulations, appreciable areas of grazing were lost owing to heavy wear by vehicles. Some of the reseeded areas were crossed from side to side and end to end with car tracks, and during peak holiday periods the numbers of vehicles parked on them made it extremely difficult for the ponies to graze what little grass was left. The commoners feel, with some justification, that the total grazing area is constantly being eroded, first by the fencing and gridding of the boundaries, then by the admittedly very necessary fencing of the main roads, and now by the building of a not inconsiderable number of car parks.

The motorists bring other less obvious problems. In spite of warning notices that the practice is illegal, visitors persist in feeding the ponies, and in doing so not only encourage them to haunt the roads and verges, where they are in grave danger from passing traffic, but deter them from looking for more natural foodstuffs. It is generally thought that some of the poorest ponies are those that stay near the roads. In addition, ponies that have come to expect titbits can become greedy and bad-tempered to the extent of biting and kicking if no food is given to them.

The most serious aspect of motoring within the area is the appalling number of animals killed and injured in accidents each year. In 1974 114 ponies died on the roads (the majority at night) and it is a disturbing fact that eighty-seven local motorists, who cannot possibly plead ignorance of the conditions, were among the offenders. The fencing of the main roads ensures that the carnage is not greater, and the action taken by the verderers and the Forestry Commission to keep roadside verges clear of high gorse and herbage has certainly kept down the number of accidents on the unfenced roads. The commoners' animals have the right of way over vehicles on the roads, as by Right of Common they are free to roam anywhere on the open Forest, and occasionally a pony exercises this right quite forcibly. One story tells of a motorist who was pushing his impatient way much too fast through a herd of ponies, with horn blaring and engine revving. As he bumped one mare out of the way, she quickly turned, lashed out with both hind feet, and left two lovely hoof marks, one on the front and one on the rear door of the offending vehicle.

The deepest and possibly the most intractable conflicts, however, arise between the commoners and those naturalists and conservationists who rightly see the New Forest as a unique area encompassing a wide range of habitats and containing an unusual number of rare plants and animals, which they believe should be preserved at almost any cost. Each side accuses the other of unwillingness to compromise, though it must be said that some of the commoners' suggestions for improving grazing are less than sound from a long-term scientific view point, and, if carried out, could actually be detrimental to their animals.

There are repeated demands, for example, for the total eradication of bracken; it is only a minor food source, provides shade for some animals but harbours many insects that irritate the ponies, and has recently come under suspicion as a possible cause of cancer. It is a fact that, over a number of years, a thick layer of litter has built up under the bracken, and this effectively prevents the growth of any ground layer of palatable grasses. Complete removal would, of course, allow these grasses to grow, but there is an alternative, which could be to the ponies' advantage. If the bracken could be systematically swiped in the autumn (as it used be years ago, when large quantities were used for bedding), this would prevent the build-up of litter and allow the growth of grasses and other ground flora during the spring and summer. More importantly, the grasses would be partially covered by the relatively thin layer of bracken throughout the summer when there is, in any case, sufficient pasture more readily available. With the coming of autumn, when food is beginning to grow scarce, the bracken dies down – and this would reveal a virtually untouched source of grass. In this way the ponies would benefit, and the important flora and fauna associated with bracken would remain untouched. Whether this is practical financially is arguable, although, with straw at its present price, bracken as bedding is almost certain to regain some of its former popularity.

Another bone of contention is the amount of burning off done within the Forest. The Forestry Commission has a statutory obligation to keep the grazing clear of coarse herbage, scrub, and self-sown trees, and this is partly achieved by a planned burning programme, which the commoners would like to see greatly extended. They argue that in the old days, when far greater areas were burnt, no lasting harm was done, the grazing was improved, and the spread of self-sown Scots pine prevented. A fair proportion of burning many years ago was done by 'commoners' fires' – those started without authority and supposed to be accidental! That type of burning has for the most part stopped, not because the commoners have become more careful or been converted to controlled burning, but because the Forestry Commission has facilities for reaching most illegal blazes much more quickly. Some burning is undoubtedly beneficial. For instance, an area of heather on poorly draining subsoil will tend to have a fairly high proportion of important food grasses, such as *Molinia*, and a fire through this will normally result in an early *Molinia* flush the following April, when food is scarce (thus increasing the length of the growing season); and that grass will probably become at least sub-dominant until once again shaded out by the heather canopy. Burning also probably helps kill off parasites, and the charcoal the ponies are seen eating may act as a worm dose at a time when worming by owners cannot be performed under present methods. From the naturalist's point of view, however, the burning of heather over a wide area would be disastrous, as the interesting flora and fauna of this particular habitat are richer in mature heathland than in younger growth.

The burning of gorse also has its controversial aspect. In the New Forest gorse and associated heathland are of great importance as the habitats of the rare Dartford warbler, as well as a number of other interesting animals, and any further diminution must be viewed with disquiet. Again the more mature areas are the richest, and burning will inevitably alter the balance in favour of younger stands. On the other hand, gorse aged between 15–20 years becomes 'leggy' and eventually dies out, and denuding an area of this important plant would be a disaster for the ponies. Burning, properly controlled, can aid gorse regeneration, although its growth is restricted by the browsing of both ponies and cattle.

Although a number of ponies lose their lives in Forest bogs, few commoners would want to see these areas completely drained, as this would destroy large amounts of *Molinia* grass. They would, however, like to see measures taken to prevent old bogs enlarging and new ones forming through the flooding of lawns (which tend to revert to bog). They would also like a more satisfactory method of drainage disposal from the inclosures, to stop the fouling of the edges that sometimes occurs at present. The problems to be dealt with are exceedingly complex. The difficult task of working towards a balance between the needs of commoners, naturalists, and all the other groups using the Forest, lies in the hands of the verderers, the Commoners' Defence Association, the Forestry Commission, and the Nature Conservancy Council. The future of the ponies and the New Forest itself is up to them.

3

DAILY LIFE IN THE FOREST

HAUNTS AND HERDS

Although the ponies are free to roam more or less at will throughout the 47,000 acres or so of open Forest, the commoners must be able to round up their animals from time to time, to select those for sale, to inspect their condition, or to provide veterinary treatment if necessary, and it might seem an impossible task to find a particular animal among the 3,000 odd grazing in such a vast area. Fortunately the habits of the ponies themselves make this a much less daunting task than would at first appear.

A pony born and bred on the Forest can indeed wander unrestricted, but it normally stays within a fairly well defined area known as its haunt. Most ponies will stay within the haunt used by generations of ancestors. One born away from the Forest but subsequently turned out, or one moved early in life, may 'haunt in' in the immediate vicinity, or it may wander some considerable distance before settling down into an area where it will probably spend the rest of its life.

Ponies are gregarious animals who form themselves into groups of up to thirty or forty. Within the large group are smaller ones, sometimes consisting of members of a single family – granddams, dams, daughters and sisters – built up by successive generations of fillies staying in the haunt of their birth. The smaller groups are close knit, with members tending to stay within sight of each other when grazing, but not necessarily within sight of the remainder of the larger group. Nevertheless the larger group will stay within the confines of its haunt. From time to time disturbances

26

may cause the animals to scatter outside their normal range. For instance, the arrival of a hunt invariably leads to a great deal of excited galloping around with little regard to the distance travelled, as do the annual round-ups. During the breeding season individual mares may be forced to leave the group if they are rejected by the resident stallion, and others will return to a previous haunt to foal.

Sometimes a lone mare will appear, using the same haunt but never quite part of the herd. More often than not this animal will graze out of sight of the group, but will nonetheless follow the same patterns of movement within the prescribed area as the other ponies. The foal of a loner frequently inherits its dam's independent habits, grazing not only some distance from the group but a considerable way from its mother at a very early age, only returning to her for milk. This is in direct contrast to normal behaviour, in which a foal rarely moves more than about 25yd from its dam during the first week of life, and at 5 months of age will still spend nearly 90 per cent of its time within 50yd of the mare.

In groups of animals there is usually a distinct hierarchy, and this is quite plainly seen within herds of ponies. Generally speaking among fully adult mares, size determines the individual's place in the table of dominance rather than age. The dominant mare within the group will often be the one to begin the move to fresh grazing, and when hay is put out as supplementary feeding during the winter, the order of precedence is made very clear by threatening behaviour, ranging from a mere flattening of the ears to a full-scale two-heeled kick. The position of the stallions within the groups is less easy to establish. Their numbers are strictly controlled and the conditions under which they live on the Forest are somewhat artificial. A number are left out throughout the year, while others are out from May until September or October only, and it is part of the management policy to move them to different districts at least every four years. During the breeding season each stallion will dominate his group of mares, rounding them up to prevent them straying or being stolen by a rival, but he is by no means always the one to lead a move to fresh grazing. Those left out all the year almost certainly take precedence when hay is supplied. Two- or three-year-old colts are normally dominated by both stallions and older mares, unless they happen to be the only males in an area during the breeding season.

The areas of the haunts the herds inhabit vary widely. One group, some of whose members are hand-fed during the winter, haunts a comparatively small area round a commoner's small-holding; it has never been known to move more than half a mile away in any direction. Other groups may have much more extensive haunts, extending upwards of 3 miles from a central point. But small or large, the haunt will have within its boundaries everything a pony needs to survive – food, water, and shelter from the wind, sun, rain, and forest flies. Once settled a pony only occasionally leaves its haunt voluntarily, and this of course is a great boon to the owner, who knows where he can expect to find his animals. It must be said, however, that knowing where to look is one thing but finding an animal is sometimes quite another. As one commoner remarked with feeling: 'The fact that you can't find a pony doesn't mean it isn't there – it's just that you can't see it.' The Foresters are past masters at creeping into the deep woods or hiding among high gorse bushes to avoid being caught.

The commoners have their own opinions about the merits or otherwise of particular haunts. Some they describe as bad – those, for example, which include the verges along busy roads, with the ever-present danger of accidents, or take in one of the many disused gravel pits scattered throughout the Forest. Although in time grass and gorse grow over the old workings, the hard ground puts an unnatural strain on the ponies' feet, and constant grazing over a gravelly surface wears down their teeth until, in extreme cases, bottom and top teeth no longer meet. Haunts regarded as good are those away from busy roads, on ground that does not damage the feet and teeth, and offering a satisfactory range of food plants and shelter.

In spite of their condemnation of some haunts, the commoners are reluctant to move ponies away from them. Its haunt is very important to a pony; some are thoroughly upset if removed, and will fret and lose condition quite quickly. Others, if brought in for veterinary treatment or special feeding, will refuse to cooperate, and in rare cases have been known to lie down and die. If not safely confined, they may jump out of fields or yards, and in spite of the fact that they have probably been brought in by trailer or lorry, will manage to find their way back to their haunt within a very few days. One stallion was observed running up and down the fencing along the A31 road through the Forest until it found an underpass through which it could reach home. Indeed there are so many stories of ponies finding their way from one end of the Forest to the other across country they could not possibly know, that there seems reason to doubt the view generally accepted by scientists that horses do not have a true homing instinct.

The movement of ponies within their haunts appears to be controlled by such factors as the season, the time of day or night, the weather and the availability of food and water. Ponies seem to know instinctively when bad weather is on the way, and hours before a storm arrives they usually leave open ground for shelter, either among trees or high gorse, or close to roadside hedges. Conversely, if at dusk the ponies are seen high on the plateaux, it is a fair indication of a fine night to come. Seasonal variations in pony sightings can be quite marked. Casual observers see a great many more ponies on the Forest in the summer and conclude that many must therefore have been turned out after spending the winter on the holdings. This is only partly true. Some certainly are turned out for the summer, but a considerable number join them from the heart of the deep woods or gorse brakes, which form their winter quarters. Only with the return of warmer weather and the first signs of the new season's grass will these latter ponies emerge, giving the impression that many more have suddenly been turned out.

SHADES

During the summer the most striking feature of the ponies' routine is their use of 'shades' – areas in which large herds or small groups collect, not to escape the sun, as one might think from the word itself, but the swarms of vicious biting Forest flies. Almost predictably, the ponies shade in traditional places, and these too vary with the time of day and the month. A favourite site in the north of the area is Fritham Aerodrome, a relic of World War II now mostly grassed over but retaining some of the concrete runways. In June ponies come from as far afield as Linwood (some 3 to 4 miles distant) to stand together in groups on the runways or on the open grassy plain away from the coarse herbage that attracts flies.

At this time of year, for some reason, ponies are strongly attracted to bare open ground. The usual explanation put forward is that they are seeking the breeze which discourages flies, but this is probably only one of several reasons. Often the ponies shade in comparatively still air some 50yd or more from an area with much stronger air currents – one that would seem much more suitable. Other ponies choose tarmac roads for their shades: at one spot along the Cadnam-Fordingbridge road a dozen or more can be seen day after day, standing steadfastly in the middle of the road and holding up traffic in both directions, until some irate motorist finally loses patience and gets out to chase them away. Even then they usually move just far enough to allow the cars through in one direction, and then return to block the road once more. This shade may certainly be in the middle of a strong air current, but if that was the ponies' sole criterion, it might be thought that standing by the *side* of the road, where they would catch the considerable breeze from passing cars, would be more beneficial. An alternative suggestion is that roadway shades are attractive because the petrol and diesel fumes act as insect deterrents.

As the summer progresses into July and August, some of the ponies that have hitherto shaded in the open move into the woods. Here too they tend to return to the same tree or groups of trees year after year, though they may congregate round one tree one day and another the next. In unsettled or thundery weather, especially if it comes towards the end of August, some will shade in bracken, standing quietly in small groups with their heads down among the fronds.

As in most other activities, the ponies' movements in and out of shade conform to a fairly regular timetable. They go into shade, be it in the open or under the trees, as soon as the sun begins to get hot in the morning. During the day they leave from time to time for water, pausing to snatch a few quick mouthfuls of food on the way there and back. They are not away long, returning usually at the trot. In the late afternoon, as the sun is sinking, they move off to their traditional night-time grazing grounds, chiefly in the valley bottoms.

The regular habits of the ponies were put to good use by one old and exceedingly patient commoner who wanted to catch up one of his mares. Knowing that she shaded under a certain tree, he arrived in the early morning before the group returned from night grazing. Equipped with a ring-rope (a rope with a noose at one end which can be guided over the pony's head by means of a long stick or pole), he climbed the tree and sat patiently waiting until the ponies came along. Even when they arrived, his vigil was not over, because he had to wait until the mare he wanted stood precisely underneath him. Then he quickly guided the rope over her head and round her neck, slipped out the pole, and that was that.

Although generations of ponies have probably used the same shades, they are extraordinarily resourceful animals, not slow to take advantage of man-made facilities. After World War II many derelict army huts were left round the various Forest aerodromes and it was not long before the ponies were using some of them as shades. In many ways they were ideal, but occasionally their use ended in tragedy. The animals would go into the huts and, as ponies will, rub up against some protruding object to relieve an itch. Alas, the protruding object was sometimes the door, which closed, trapping the animals inside to die a miserable death from starvation if no one found them in time. An even more modern adaptation followed the fencing of the A31 trunk road in 1963–4. To allow ponies access to their haunts on both sides of the road, as well as to provide safe crossing places for riders and walkers, a number of concrete underpasses were constructed. Within a very short time the animals' natural curiosity, coupled with their instinctive desire to move from one part of their territory to another, led them to investigate these new structures. They discovered that the underpasses made ideal shades, and these are now so popular with both ponies and cattle that animals spill out at each end. Not all the underpasses are used, and it has been suggested that those approached through woods are rejected because the ponies will not willingly pass through the massive swarms of flies and other insects that congregate among the trees.

4

FEEDING

As most of the ponies' day during high summer is spent in shade, often in places where there is little or no food, the bulk of their feeding must take place during the night. In the late afternoon or early evening they may be seen streaming out of their shades and heading purposefully along tracks worn bare by generations of ponies towards the bottoms of the many valleys that intersect the higher plateaux of the Forest. Usually they plod steadily along with their heads held low, often in single file; but on occasions, as they start to go down hill, they break into a trot and suddenly, as if celebrating the cool of the evening after a long hot day, give a few exuberant bucks and squeals and gallop down to the valley bottom. There they spend the night eating large quantities of purple moor grass (*Molinia caerulea*), which grows in and around the valley bogs. Some spend the night in the woods, grazing on the grassy 'lawns' of *Agrostis and Festuca*, but the main food plant during the summer is undoubtedly *Molinia*.

As the year wears on towards autumn, less time is spent in shade, and more ponies can be seen along roadside verges or on the lawns beside the numerous streams, and on the open stretches of grassland known as the reseeded areas. These areas, originally covered by coarse grasses, gorse and bracken, were ploughed and sown with an improved mixture of grasses during and after World War II in a deliberate effort to improve the quality of grazing. The scheme might have been more successful had stock been prevented from grazing until the new crop was firmly established, but, as it is, in most cases the indigenous grasses such as fine bent sheep's fescue, and in some places rye grass, have become dominant. Nevertheless the gorse and bracken have not returned, and the reseeded areas, although amounting to rather less than 900 acres, form an important part of the grazing for ponies and cattle throughout the year.

At various times during the summer certain ponies can be seen up to their bellies in the ponds or water-filled bomb craters scattered throughout the Forest, or plodding slowly along some of the drainage ditches. They are feeding on species of water plants such as water sweet grass (*Glyceria* spp), and the shoots of sedges, rushes and bur-reeds (*Sparganium* spp). The many large tracts of bracken also provide a certain amount of food, and although the foals seem particularly fond of the young tender shoots, older animals usually leave the plant until it is fully grown, and not long before it begins to change colour in the autumn. Although extensive areas of the New Forest are covered with ling (*Calluna vulgaris*) and heather (*Erica* spp), these, rather surprisingly perhaps, do not form a major part of the ponies' diet, although some are eaten during the winter. Bramble leaves and shoots are a favourite food, and the young shoots of broad-leaved trees such as oak and beech are browsed with evident enjoyment, as is a certain amount of ivy. It is in the winter, however, when all the available grass has been eaten, that the feeding of the New Forest ponies enters its most interesting stage.

GORSE EATERS

Almost as soon as the first frost comes, many animals leave their summer grazing grounds and move into the areas of gorse (or fuzz, as it is called locally) found in nearly all haunts. Some of the older bushes are 6 or 7ft tall, and entering one of these dense brakes is not unlike going into a maze. Narrow tracks lead in and out between the bushes, often terminating in dead ends, and it is quite possible to hear a pony, and even to see its head a few yards away, and yet be quite unable to find a way through to it. Obviously fuzz provides admirable shelter from wind and rain, but more importantly it provides one of the chief winter foods. Being leguminous, it is highly nutritious.

Plate 5 Three of the New Forest verderers inspecting a colt before it is permitted to run out on the Forest; (from left to right) Miss Dionis Macnair, Mr Hugh Pasmore, Mr Gerald Forward

Plate 6 Ponies shading on the open Forest, in the breeze and away from flies

Plate 7 Colt-hunting in the New Forest by Lucy Kemp-Welch, which gives an excellent idea of present-day colt-hunting

Plate 8 Verderer Hugh Pasmore and his wife tailing a colt

It is a fascinating sight to watch gorse eaters (the commoners call them fuzz toppers) dealing with this prickly meal. They eat the tips (which have a particularly high protein content), and when they have selected a shoot, they roll back their upper lip and to a lesser extent their lower and carefully bite through the stem. Then, with lips still apart and mouths slightly open, they gently manoeuvre the mouthful back until they can chew it with their grinding teeth. If they are feeding from small bushes, they often paw the gorse with their forefeet, apparently to soften it and perhaps break some of the spines. Towards the end of the winter the gorse begins to flower, and it is not uncommon, although at first rather startling, to come face to face with a pony whose lips and muzzle are bright yellowy-green from the flower juices.

Some Foresters are, it is believed, unique in having two physical characteristics that can only be interpreted as adaptations to feeding on gorse. One is the extraordinary moustache grown by some on their upper lips (see plate, p 18), and the less notice-able beard on the lower jaws. The other is the unusual thickness and toughness of the upper surface of some ponies' tongues. The beards are quite soft thick hair up to 3in long, and make some ponies' heads appear to be larger than average. Moustaches, which seem to be not very common these days, vary markedly from area to area, probably depending on the amount of gorse eaten. For example, there is a small herd on Gorley Hill, where there is a high concentration of gorse, in which all the animals, including the stallion, show some signs of moustaches, whereas in another area where there is less gorse, not a single one may be seen. A sugges-tion that only the more common-bred ponies grow them was more or less conclusively disproved by one of the most successful stallions ever to be bred on the Forest – Mrs E. H. Parsons's Deeracres Winston Churchill. He was a magnificent animal and a prolific prize winner, who every winter sported a splendid moustache. Fortunately for his show career, as soon as he was brought in for the summer season, he used to rub it off on his manger! There is, however, probably some truth in the view that the older type of pony with a moustache is gradually being bred out. It is also possible that the pony society's present policy of encouraging commoners to take foals away from mares and winter them in may have something to do with it.

It is not known at what stage the ponies develop the tough tongues and moustaches, but they are certainly not born with them. Some experts believe that unless the foals remain with their dams for the winter, they may never learn to eat gorse, and it is certainly true that if they are turned out again after the first winter, they do not usually grow any form of protection. Not enough is known about this subject at present, although it is known that if an older mare is brought off the Forest, her moustaches will disappear within two or three years.

The protective hair also doubtless helps the ponies when they eat holly (their other main winter food), although they prefer the smooth-leaved variety if they can reach it. It is most noticeable that nearly all mature holly bushes have a distinct browse line, about 8ft from the ground, below which the leaves are virtually stripped. During the bad winter of 1962-3 large holly trees were felled to provide additional food and it was observed that the ponies bit off the leaves from behind, thus avoiding the worst of the prickles. At that time, when the trees were on the ground, not only did they eat all the leaves but they stripped the bark as well, and all that was left were great white skeletons of boughs lying in the snow.

FEEDING DANGERS

The ponies are not always quite so sensible about their feeding; each autumn they gorge themselves on fallen acorns, and a significant number succumb to acorn poisoning, about which very little is known. Feeding habits can also lead to a different kind of tragedy. Most Foresters are quite accustomed to the numerous bogs throughout their habitats, and know where they can walk in safety; but in the early spring grass often comes through first in the bogs and boggy drains, and when the hungry animals try to reach it, down they go. Their frantic struggles to escape only result in their sinking deeper and deeper. As the surface is disturbed, the underlying water comes up and forms a pool round their heads, and they quickly drown. These tragedies occur all too frequently, serving to illustrate that life in the Forest can be harsh in the extreme.

LANE-CREEPERS

The feeding habits of a great many ponies were forcibly changed in 1963-4, when the whole of the New Forest was fenced and cattle grids were installed on every road crossing its boundaries. Before this, Foresters were able to move without restrictions over a wide area outside the official boundaries. They grazed the road-side verges, and made nuisances of themselves by jumping into farmers' fields and private gardens, and were, of course, a menace on the roads. Probably the only people who welcomed them were the local authorities, as they kept the verges neatly mown. All the surrounding towns were forced to maintain pounds, and when the ponies became too much of an annoyance, a round-up was held, the nearest agister told, and the commoners had to collect their property on payment of a fine.

One famous and regular occupant of Ringwood pound was Broomy Slipon – now regarded as one of the foundation stallions of the post-war breed. He used to spend most of his winters in the back gardens of the town, and was a great favourite with the children, standing placidly while one clambered on his back, and allowing another to lead him by the forelock. It goes without saying, however, that immediately Slipon and his wandering friends were put back on the Forest, they turned round and headed back down the lanes in search of the good life again. Their habit of haunting the roads earned them the name of 'lane-creepers', and generally speaking they were able to maintain themselves in much better condition than their stay-at-home relatives.

The owners of lane-creepers, exasperated by regular summonses and fines for allowing ponies to stray on the highway, and the nuisance of having to collect them from the pounds, tried numerous methods of restraint. Some commoners tried hobbles, but the ponies, resourceful as always, learned to gallop with the hobbles still on. Another owner tried putting chains round the ponies' necks and tethering them on the open Forest, but this was frus-trated by 'do-gooders' who took pity on them and pulled up the tether pegs. Off went the ponies down the lanes again, dragging the chains behind them – or worse, made off into the woods, where the chains became caught up and the ponies were not only lost but trapped. Unless they were found, they starved to death. In 1937 the pony society held a special sale at Beaulieu Road yards of lane-creepers; this was a considerable success from the owners' point of view, but was not repeated, as the auctioneers made a loss.

FOREST ECOLOGY

The feeding habits of the ponies are bound up with those of the two other large herbivores on the Forest – deer and cattle. The three are vital to each other if a grazing balance is to be maintained. If there are too few cattle, for example, the spread of coarse herbage and young self-sown trees accelerates, thus depriving the ponies and deer of some grazing areas, and similarly without the deer and cattle, fewer ponies could be kept. The number of cattle varies, but rose from about 1,600 in 1971 (probably too few as far as the ponies were concerned) to over 3,000 in 1974 (almost certainly too many). A figure of just under 3,000 is thought to be about right for the present number of ponies, provided the cattle are dispersed and not kept in herds of 300 or more, as is inclined to be the case. During most winters a significant proportion of cattle are removed, so that direct competition for food at the most critical time is possibly not so great as the figures might suggest. Also cattle do not browse to the same extent as ponies. During the winter of 1974–5, owing to the rise in fodder prices, more cattle than ever before were left out, and if this trend continues, a very serious situation could result.

The presence of the commoners' animals in the Forest obviously affects its ecology, and has done so for hundreds of years. Grazing and browsing over the centuries has shown not only to have restricted the natural regeneration of the woodlands but also largely to have eliminated such palatable species as elm, lime and hazel, whose new shoots were nibbled away. The restriction of woodland regeneration has allowed the maintenance of heathland, acid grassland and open areas, and were it not for constant grazing, these areas would soon revert to scrub and then to woods once more. Thus, but for the animals, the appearance and nature of the New Forest would have undergone fundamental changes, and a number of valuable ecological features would disappear.

5

THE PONIES' WELL-BEING

The ponies bred on the Forest are a tough hardy race, but their general physical condition over the years has been a never-ending source of criticism, argument, and – it must be said – misunderstanding and ignorance. Many people, both residents and visitors, are horrified at the appearance of some of the mares, and the oft-heard remarks about 'walking skeletons' and 'bags of bones' are all too often true, particularly at the end of the winter. The verderers, the agisters, and especially the commoners have all come in for their share of blame for these pitiful looking animals but unfortunately the most strident criticism has come from a vocal minority who do not fully understand the problems or the limitations of the legal methods available to deal with them. These uninformed attacks have tended to overshadow the more constructive suggestions of knowledgeable critics. In the past some of the verderers and agisters may have been less than conscientious, and it is undeniable that a number of commoners do not appear to care about the condition of their ponies. But the majority of people concerned with the ponies' welfare – verderers, commoners and agisters – do care. They accept that there is still room for improvement, and they are taking a variety of measures to deal with criticisms.

CARE OF PONIES

It is widely accepted that the condition of the ponies suffered a setback when the Forest was fenced and gridded in the 1960s. Within a short space of time hundreds of lane-creepers, who had been finding a very good living outside the perambulations, were suddenly confined within them. This was not so serious during the summer, when grazing was probably adequate for the population, but towards the end of the winter there was insufficient good food for the increased number of animals. Many lane-creepers had, in all probability, become so accustomed to a comparatively rich and readily available food supply outside the Forest that they had lost the ability to search for and exist on much sparser pastures to which they were now restricted. This situation has been exacerbated in succeeding years by the fact that the total number of animals (ponies, cattle, pigs and donkeys) depastured increased from approximately 4,500 to 6,700 in 1974. An obvious solution would be to limit the number of animals turned out, but, because of the Right of Common of Pasture, the verderers do not have the power to do this.

An important move was made in 1965, when the verderers set up a Veterinary Surgeons' Consultative Committee consisting of local practitioners, who give generously of their time and knowledge. The Committee's function is to investigate and make recommendations on various aspects of the animals' welfare. For the last few winters members of the Committee have undertaken monthly tours of inspection of the ponies, pointing out to the agister in each district which type of pony should be taken off and which allowed to stay. In these inspections the time of year is taken very much into consideration. For instance, the type of animal that is poor (or plain, as the commoners call it) at the beginning of winter is viewed much more seriously than that which is poor towards spring and would normally be expected to pick up with the advent of the new season's grass. The veterinary surgeons' role in these inspections is purely advisory, and it is not their function to order the removal of individual animals; but their advice is much appreciated by the verderers and agisters.

It is the verderers' responsibility, through the agisters, to order individual animals off the Forest, and even this is not so straightforward as might appear. Most commoners are cooperative, indeed grateful, when advised by the agister that one of their animals is poor, and will take steps to remove it as soon as possible. Strictly speaking, however, the verderers only have the power to order the removal of an animal that is actually suffering. For example, if a mare with a foal at foot is looking a bit poor at the start of the winter, the verderers are likely to advise the owner that he can leave the mare on, provided he takes the foal off; otherwise both should be removed. But a commoner who insists on sticking to the letter of the law could quite legally refuse to remove the foal, because it was not being caused suffering by remaining on the mare. In such an instance both could stay on the Forest until the mare was such a bag of bones that the verderers were able to enforce its removal. Fortunately, most commoners act on the advice given to them, although there have been allegations from time to time that ponies have been removed as instructed and almost immediately turned out in a different area.

The removal of ponies from the Forest can in itself present difficulties. Most animals become poorest towards the end of the winter and in the early spring, when many mares are heavy in foal and a few even have very young foals at foot. It is often necessary to chase a pony to catch it, and it is at least debatable whether more serious damage is not done to a larger number of in-foal mares by pursuing then in the course of catching one poor one than in leaving the latter alone. Furthermore few outsiders can appreciate that the time lapse can quite legitimately be considerable between a pony first being reported or observed and its removal. First the agister must catch it up (unless it is already known to him) to identify its brand. He must then notify the owner, who, if he has a weekday employment away from the Forest, may only be able to look for it at the weekend, by which time it will almost certainly have moved from where it was when reported. Some ponies take days, and even weeks, to find. Once found, it must be caught – and a really clever wild pony that knows every bog, bush and tree in its haunt can be frustratingly difficult to catch. A favourite ploy is to gallop, apparently quite deliberately, into a boggy patch where riders dare not follow, or to disappear into dark dense woodland. Sometimes the weather plays a part, with icy conditions, say, effectively preventing riders from galloping their ponies during a chase.

Although it would seem desirable to remove poor animals from the Forest, an increasing number of knowledgeable people are questioning its advisability, unless it is certain that the move will be to their advantage. Disturbing reports have suggested that conditions on some of the holdings or grazing to which these animals are removed are infinitely worse than any to be found on the Forest. In the winter of 1974–5 owners simply could not afford to buy hay at up to £100 a ton, and stories have been told of ponies confined to bare muddy fields, with only a bit of mouldy hay or straw to pick at. Reliable witnesses have described ponies so poor that they had to be held up by two men; and unless the price of fodder comes down, this situation is likely to be repeated.

Many factors contribute to the poor condition of some ponies. Age, of course, is important, and the older mares are most likely to lose condition, owing to a declining ability to digest food properly, poor teeth, and a general run-down in the body processes with age. Over the past few years the pony society secretary, Miss Macnair, has been keeping an eye on the incidence of parrot mouths and undershot jaws in the stallions inspected by the verderers, and has compiled some very interesting figures. Since 1970, 360 stallions (of all ages) have been passed, but twenty-two have been rejected because of parrot mouth. Seven two-year-olds were required to be re-examined when they had a full mouth, and the four of these that were re-presented all passed. This does suggest that youngsters jaws tend to re-align with maturity. In 1975 twenty-four stallions were passed, five were rejected for parrot mouth or undershot jaws, and one is to be re-examined at maturity – a rate of 20 per cent defective. If this rate is repeated among the mares on the Forest (which are not subject to compulsory veterinary checks), it could explain the poor condition of a significant number, especially among the two- and three-year-olds before their mouths have matured. It might also explain the puzzling variation in condition between animals using the same grazing areas, as the ones with badly aligned teeth would clearly be at a disadvantage. These figures have only just become available, and any remedial action has yet to be discussed, but they do illustrate the constant attention given by the verderers and others to the ponies' welfare.

BREEDING PROBLEMS

One of the most controversial questions affecting the ponies is the type and size of animals that economic conditions over the last decade or so have encouraged some commoners to try and breed. It is generally accepted that big better-bred ponies (anything over about 13·1 hands) are less hardy and adaptable than the small, not very beautiful but extremely tough, runty little Foresters, which get down in the bogs and look well winter and summer. Larger ponies need more food, and have a greater surface area from which to lose heat. (There are, of course, exceptions, for some bigger animals are known to thrive and some smaller ones need to be brought in. The only explanation for this is that some ponies are of a hardier strain than others.) When the demand for riding ponies both at home and overseas was heavy, the temptation to breed larger animals to meet this profitable market was enormous. Rather better quality stallions, which could not necessarily be left out all the year, were used, and a better foal often resulted. Provided that foal was sold off the Forest (as would normally be the case with colts), no lasting harm was done; but if the bigger, better looking fillies were left on as brood mares, with the idea of producing a line of quality foals, the chances of their quickly losing condition were infinitely greater. When prices are high, the fact that some of these mares need to be taken off and hand-fed need not be a financial disaster for the owners. However, when sale prices drop and the cost of feeding escalates (as in 1974 and 1975), an increasing number of mares that should be taken off before the winter are left out, only to be ordered off later when their poor condition demands it.

It is conflicts of interests such as this that lead to accusations (sometimes justified) that some commoners want it all ways – they expect good quality mares to produce better foals and also do well throughout the winter with a foal at foot and carrying another. Unfortunately, with few exceptions, this ideal cannot be achieved under Forest conditions.

INFESTATION AND FLIES

One of the other significant influences on the condition of the ponies is infestation by worms – both red (*Stronglyus* spp) and white (*Ascaroids*). The red worms are the more dangerous and debilitating, as they feed directly from their host's blood stream thus depriving the pony of material on which it has expended precious energy processing. Round worms, although larger and more frightening in appearance, feed on material in the animal's gut before it is fully digested, or even on waste that would normally pass straight through. Red worm infestation is much higher in young ponies, since the older ones apparently build up some resistance to it over the years. Counts done by the Veterinary Committee showed that the mean for yearlings was 1,500 per gram of faeces (1,000 per gram is considered clinically significant), whereas the mean in adult mares was 776 per gram, although in some cases it rose as high as 6,950 per gram.

Treating semi-wild ponies on the Forest for worms has obvious difficulties, but in the late 1960s a scheme was introduced by the Commoners' Defence Association whereby worming powders and liquids are obtainable at reduced prices, and animals are wormed at the only time of the year when this is possible – at the annual drifts. Owners have taken enthusiastic advantage of this scheme, and in 1974 enough worming material was sold to treat every pony on the Forest, although some, of course, may have been used for animals on the holdings. It has been suggested that worming once a year is inadequate, and that in time the parasites will develop immunity; but, as a veterinary surgeon pointed out, getting rid of a mass of worms even once a year gives the body defences a chance to build up resistance, and this must be beneficial. Some ponies are, of course, wormed more than once a year. Those that are normally taken off for the winter are often wormed on the holdings, as are some of those that are ordered off. The worming programme is certainly a big advance in pony management, but the basic problem of highly infected grazing still remains to be tackled.

The ponies are plagued by a variety of other invertebrate pests.

Ticks are prevalent throughout the summer months, especially around the heads and necks, and lice gather in the manes during the winter. Both these cause the ponies to scratch and rub against trees and other solid objects, and are probably one reason for the mutual grooming that takes place so often. Birds such as jack-daws and magpies are sometimes observed perching on the animals' backs and pecking around the mane in search of para-sites. New Forest flies or keds (*Hipposbosca equinea*) infect the tail region in the spring, causing a great deal of irritation to foals but little apparently to adults. Throughout the spring and summer mosquitoes and biting midges (*Culicoides* spp), black fly (*Simulium equinum*), and several species of biting and non-biting flies attack the ponies, and are at least partly responsible for the daily move-ment to shade. A more dramatic effect sometimes results from the loud buzzing of Tabanid flies, when groups of ponies suddenly take off and gallop wildly about. An old story tells of commoners catching some of the more vicious Forest flies, putting them in matchboxes, and releasing them at one of the more important local shows. Not surprisingly, pandemonium broke loose among the 'foreign' ponies not accustomed to such insects, while the Foresters stood firm, behaved beautifully, and carried off the prizes!

DISEASES AND INJURIES

The ponies, although hardy, do fall victim to infectious diseases such as strangles, which is nearly always present somewhere in the Forest. From time to time, depending on the strain of the bacter-ium, a more serious outbreak occurs, resulting in some deaths and possibly a number of slipped foals. Flu epidemics also hit the area periodically, causing a great deal of coughing but apparently not doing any lasting harm.

The most serious complaint is acorn poisoning, which is all the more serious because it is so little understood. Each autumn a varying number of cases occur, but no distinct pattern has emerged, and although the incidence is usually less in a poor acorn year, it does not necessarily follow that a heavy crop produces a proportional increase in poisoning. Nevertheless, during October and November each year, anything up to fifty ponies die, and the numbers have gone up to over 100 in a particularly bad year. The animals often leave their normal feeding grounds to grub among fallen acorns in the woods, and many find their way into the fenced Forestry Commission inclosures. Nearly all eat acorns greedily, and some gorge on them year after year without apparent ill effect; indeed a pony that can eat them safely thrives and faces the winter in better than average condition. Others, however, succumb quickly.

A local veterinary surgeon who attends many cases each year describes the symptoms of acute acorn poisoning as severe diarrhoea, often with haemorrhage, temperatures as high as 106°F, a pulse of over 100 and rapid general collapse. He believes the causative agent may be an alkaloid. Post-mortem examination shows a remarkable degree of bowl oedoma (a form of watery swelling) and haemorrhagic enteritis (inflammation), and large quantities of acorn husks are found. Some success in treating this form of poisoning has been achieved by the administration of drugs intravenously and intramuscularly, followed by Epsom salts given some four hours later by stomach tube. Sub-acute poisoning produces symptoms similar to constipation, probably due to husks and to tannic acid, and this may be treated by the veterinary surgeon with liquid paraffin. The chronic form, which occurs later in the year, usually at the end of November, is invariably fatal. Ponies are either found dead or staggering about, sometimes blind or in a state of coma. Post-mortem examination usually reveals liver damage.

Fortunately, other forms of food poisoning are rare in the Forest, though there are occasional instances of bracken poisoning. Colic is rare, because of the wide range of foodstuffs, but some trouble is caused by well meaning people putting out piles of grass clippings and herbaceous perennials. Grass clippings probably do less harm if spread out in a thin layer, for they quickly become heated when left in a heap and a form of fermentation sets in, producing substances likely to cause colic. Grass that has been sprayed with any form of weed-killer or similar substance is also dangerous, and some herbaceous plants are certainly toxic.

Large numbers of visitors during the summer inevitably leave large amounts of litter. The ponies, who have learnt to scavenge, occasionally eat plastic wrapping material, whose insolubility may eventually cause them a slow and lingering loss of condition. More serious, however, are the injuries caused by broken bottles and discarded tins. Severe cuts are quite common, and there have been cases of ponies stepping into tins that have become stuck, causing painful, badly infected wounds. Visitors cannot, however, be held responsible for the injuries caused by poachers' trapping wires, as the poachers are believed to be locals. Some years ago one of the agisters found a trailing wire cutting into a pony's neck to a depth of some 1½in. It must have caused the utmost pain.

One condition from which ponies on the Forest are completely free is laminitis; there is never sufficient rich food available to cause it. It is, however, a problem against which owners of ponies away from the Forest must guard. Take, for instance, the average Forester bought at Beaulieu Road. Unless it is in very hard work the pony is happiest and healthiest under conditions as near natural as possible. A field with shelter but not too much lush grass is ideal. A pony straight off the Forest will miss the variety of food available there, so supplementary food such as hay or perhaps some pony nuts should be fed according to the amount of work done. Over-feeding with oats should be avoided at all costs.

FOALING

Of the natural hazards facing the ponies, foaling might be considered the greatest, but few mares have any difficulties, chiefly because they lead a natural type of life, and are certainly never over-fat. Abortion is not unusual in equines generally, in part because of evolutionary change taking place in the placenta, and Forest mares are no exception. Some foetuses are probably lost through mares being chased at a critical time, and Nature will also take a hand if a mare is in particularly poor condition. It is not thought, however, that there is any infective condition in the area that causes abortion.

In general the mares 'do' their foals extremely well, often at their own expense, and it is not uncommon to see a poor mare with a bouncing, well grown youngster. One of the bitterest criticisms aimed at the commoners by ill informed people is that they allow their mares to foal year after year without rest – 'foal factories' is a common term employed by these critics. It is true that some mares do foal every year until they are quite old – seventeen or eighteen – but statistics show that in any one year not more than about 55 per cent of mares on the Forest produce a foal. Another common criticism is that 'foals are producing foals' – in other words, two- and three-year-old fillies are getting in foal – an occurrence that would pass almost without comment on a private stud. Although this may occasionally be true, it is rare; it was more common before the fencing and gridding were completed. Forest-bred mares do not often foal before their fourth year, and five or six is more usual. Younger mares are certainly served by stallions, but either fail to conceive or abort.

One or two strange stories have emerged over the years about the breeding habits of Forest ponies. One lady was quite convinced that they foaled twice a year – an occurrence that would surprise and delight the commoners – but the most unusual tale is one that was not only taken seriously by non-medical people at the time (1848) but was authenticated by a Salisbury doctor and by a Keeper of the Forest. It was said that a seven-months-old filly found in the Forest was a cross between a pony mare and a red stag. The dam had been seen with the deer for some months, and in due course she produced a remarkable looking offspring. (See plate, p 53). Its nose was said to resemble that of both deer and pony, its forehead was round and its feet double like a deer's, and it had a deer's tail. There is, of course, no scientific foundation for such a hybrid, but a possible explanation suggests itself. The feet are the most puzzling, but occasionally ponies are born bearing an extra digit on one leg (commonly explained as being a throwback to the ancestral bovine hoof); and it may have been that the creature described had four such feet. For the rest, one only has to look at some of the runty little yearlings or two-year-olds of the present day, especially during the winter, when their shaggy coats conceal the true body shape to a considerable extent. It is by no means unusual for youngsters to have slightly rounded foreheads, and the whole shape of the head in some is further distorted by the long thick beard under the jowl. Their tails at this age are quite short, and it is also common knowledge that ponies appear 'leggy' at various times before reaching maturity. Small wonder, then, that in the unscientific days of the mid-nineteenth century, such a mistake should have been made.

Plate 9 The sale ring at Beaulieu Road

Plate 10 A drawing from life by George Landseer of the so-called hybrid between a red stag and a Forest mare

Plate 11 The children's race in the New Forest point-to-point

Plate 12 Bridgelea Starlight and Mrs G. Cordall at the Brendon Two Gates check point in the 1975 Golden Horseshoe Ride on Exmoor. Starlight became the first native pony to win a Golden Horseshoe

6

THE COMMONERS AND THEIR PONIES

The New Forest has been likened to a huge stud farm, and the breeding, buying and selling of ponies has been an important part of local life for generations. The ancient custom for a commoner to present his young sons with a foal each is not quite dead. In the old days, by the time the sons came of age, they had, through the descendants of that first foal, their own small herds to carry on the family tradition. In this way many commoners still learn the business of pony management from a very early age, so that by the time they are grown men they have accumulated a fund of practical knowledge.

WORK OF THE AGISTERS

By its very nature the management of free-ranging stock differs from that of animals reared on farms or holdings, and it might be thought that the owners could leave them to their own devices until it is time to round them up and take the foals for sale. Unfortunately there are still some commoners who appear to do just that, and it is they and their neglected animals who attract much of the bad publicity that appears in the press from time to time. The majority of owners, however, know that ponies need supervision every month of the year. In this they are helped by the agisters. At the time of writing there are three agisters, though the numbers have varied over the years from two to four, and each is responsible for the well-being of the commoners' animals depastured within his own clearly defined area of the Forest. Agisters, who are nearly always commoners themselves, must have a thorough knowledge of their district and the animals within it. Some have a truly remarkable ability to recognise ponies at a distance, and can name them and their owners while most other people are still trying to decide if the animal is a pony or a cow.

In addition to making regular patrols of their districts and reporting ponies that need attention to their owners, agisters are on call 24 hours a day. They must be ready to go out at any hour of the day or night – to answer a police request to attend an animal injured in a road accident, to help a commoner look for a lost pony, to inspect a poor or injured animal reported by a member of the public, or to extricate animals from the difficulties they manage to get themselves into from time to time. Of these, the most common are being stuck in bogs or wedged tightly between two trees. The agisters have the authority to put down ponies they consider too badly injured to recover, and they are also empowered, under certain circumstances, to order commoners to remove sick or poor animals from the Forest. A comparatively recent innovation, which has helped them greatly, is the installation of two-way radios in their cars, by means of which they are in constant contact with the police. A great deal of their work, however, is done from the back of a pony, and they must be skilful and courageous horsemen.

Two most important jobs for the agisters are the organisation of the pony and cattle round-ups or 'drifts' and the collection of marking fees from the owners of all animals turned out on the Forest. These marking fees, which have risen from 2s/6d to £3 since the end of the war, are not rent paid for pasture (this is free under Common Rights) but are the charges made for the verderers' and agisters' services to the commoners. Not only must the agister collect the fee but by way of receipt he must mark the pony's tail by cutting or 'tail marking' it in a particular way (see p 21). Each agister has his own mark, which serves to confirm that the fee has been paid and to indicate in which district the pony has been turned out, though this is not necessarily the district in which its owner lives.

WINTER ON THE FOREST

The lives of the agisters and commoners follow a more or less regular pattern from year to year, depending on the routine of the ponies. There is no obvious point from which to start an account of a typical year, but a convenient time is after the last of the pony sales in November, when the Forest is settling down to face the rigours of the winter. Most of the year's colt foals and many fillies will have been sold off, leaving the brood mares, some stallions and a number of filly foals (as replacement brood mares); and the commoners must decide how many (if any) animals to remove for the winter. This is becoming an increasingly difficult problem. Some of the commoners are fortunate in having sufficient grazing on their holdings to support the animals taken off the Forest, while others may be able to rent land within easy reach. But a number have rented land many miles away – in the western ends of Dorset or Wiltshire, for instance – and the huge increase in transport costs is rapidly making such journeys uneconomic. It is not just the cost of transporting the ponies to their winter keep, for they must be inspected regularly, and in prolonged hard weather given extra food to keep them going. Many of the older commoners must look back longingly to earlier days when land-owners within the Forest used to advertise winter keep for ponies owned by members of the breed societies. For instance, in the annual report of the pony society for 1912, the following note appeared: 'Miss Baillie-Hamilton has offered to take ponies for winter keep at Burley Lodge for 1/– per head or at 1/6 for mare and foal per week.'

The owners remove those animals they know do not winter well, or have lost condition during the summer for any reason. The pony society encourages commoners to take off the foals they want to keep (in order to give the mares a better chance of doing well) and turn them out again in the spring, but in the light of recent discoveries some members would like the society to give this policy further consideration. In addition to the problem of whether or not the youngsters will develop moustaches, tough tongues, and the gorse-eating habit, it may be that during their

57

first vital winter, if left with their dams, they will develop various other survival mechanisms, which they may not if taken off. It could well be that the supposedly humanitarian step of removing the foal reduces its ability to survive in the long term. Again, not enough is known to be certain of this.

Another important decision has to be made about whether to supply additional foodstuffs during the winter months. This is a controversial point, and as with so many things to do with the ponies, the most obvious solution is not necessarily universally accepted as the right one. It seems self-evident, with ponies losing condition and food being in short supply at the end of the winter, that hand-feeding should be encouraged, and this is the policy of the pony society; but there are a number of respected commoners with a reputation for caring about their ponies who maintain that hand-feeding on the Forest is not only ineffective but sometimes makes matters worse. They argue that to distribute a bit of hay or straw, often of poor quality, among a herd of ponies (as the average owner does) is unlikely to be more than marginally beneficial. They say that it may, if the ponies are given sufficient, just maintain their condition, but will certainly not improve it. Veterinary opinion, however, states that even poor quality feed can be, and is, valuable, though it must be placed at the same spot at the same time each day. The ponies will come for it at that time, eat it, and then wander off to browse on natural food-stuffs such as gorse and holly; but if this pattern is broken, the animals will come to the appointed place and just stand, sometimes all day, waiting for food, and will not go off and feed naturally. In this case they could well be getting less than if they were not hand-fed at all.

The arguments continue. Although many ponies undoubtedly benefit from hand-feeding, some of the wilder mares that haunt in the more inaccessible parts and never come to be fed are in excellent condition throughout the winter. Some commoners who do not accept that feeding is beneficial prefer to take a poor pony on to the holding, worm it, feed it up on concentrates, and turn it out again in the spring. This system works well on the whole, but difficulties can arise with some of the wilder ponies, which are unaccustomed to anything but natural foodstuffs. They are often suspicious of concentrates, and sometimes even of hay, to the point of refusing to eat them, so that the commoner has little alternative but to turn them back on to the Forest after worming.

About 500 ponies are taken off the Forest in an average winter, and those that remain require regular inspection by the owner. With an increasing number of commoners seeking employment outside the area, many have to rely on the agisters to tell them about any that need attention. From January onwards special vigilance is necessary, for then most ponies, particularly the very old and the very young, start to lose condition. It is also the time when some ponies disappear into the deep woods or gorse brakes and are most difficult to find. Generally speaking, mares of five years old and over that have no foal at foot can, provided they start the winter in good shape, maintain their condition reasonably well right through until the spring. During January, if the season is wet, many develop a rain rash on their backs, even mares in good condition. Other than removing the animals to a more sheltered situation, there is little the commoner can do. In the early months of the year, when the ponies are at their weakest, they often seek out a sheltered position where even the winter sun can be quite warm. They like to lie down in these places and sometimes have not the strength to get up again. The immediate help of two or three people is needed if a pony in in this position is to be saved, and it must be sat up and its front legs pulled forward in order to help it get to its feet.

During the spring and early summer agisters and commoners alike are kept busy pulling ponies out of bogs, where they have become stuck when trying to reach the early *Molinia* grass. This is an extremely difficult and unpleasant job, often entailing the use of a Land Rover equipped with block and tackle. Provided the vehicle can come close enough, a rope may be run from it round the pony's neck just behind the ears (any further back and the neck would probably be broken), and the Land Rover driven slowly away. With luck the pony will gradually come out. If a Land Rover is not available, the animal may have to be manhandled (if enough helpers can be mustered) or hauled clear with ropes pulled by other ponies. It is often said that Forest ponies have learned not to stray into bogs, but this is not so. They are quite capable of being trapped more than once. One mare was hauled out, taken back to its owner's holding, treated for shock and water in the lung, and hand-fed until she had recovered. But the instant she was turned out, she went straight back and drowned herself in the bog next to the one from which she had been rescued.

JUDGING

The end of March and the beginning of April, when many animals are probably in their poorest condition, may seem an unlikely time to judge ponies. Nevertheless judging takes place annually for what are known as the Non-Hand-Fed or Forest-Fed classes of mares. As far as is known, this is a unique competition. All the mares must be (a) five years or over; (b) have run on the Forest continually since a yearling (unless holding a dispensation from the Council, such as injury, weaning, foals, worming etc, each case to be considered on its merits), and (c) have had at least one foal and be believed to be in foal again.

For the purposes of the competition the Forest is divided into three areas corresponding with the agisters' districts, and a judge is appointed for each. Before the class begins, owners and agisters ride out and form some idea of where the competing ponies are to be found, and then accompany the judges as they make their assessments. Prizes and premiums are awarded in each district, and the Dale Memorial Perpetual Challenge Cup is given to the best mare of all. The champion is decided by all three judges submitting their district winners to the scrutiny of their colleagues. Miss Olga Golby of Burley, who has judged the class on a number of occasions, recently commented on the very good ponies to be seen especially in the remoter parts of the Forest.

The scheme, inaugurated by the Burley Pony Society in 1911, was to encourage the breeding of good mares, able to stay in condition on the Forest. Lord Arthur Cecil and the Rev T. F. Dale, the judges of the first of these competitions, had this to say:

As this is a new departure in the judging of out native ponies, it will be well for the judges to set out before the committee the methods of judging adopted. It was desirable, to begin with, to move and disturb the ponies as little as possible, and the methods of approaching the herds was rather to stalk than to drive them. As the judges gained experience, it was found easy to approach the ponies, to walk around them and view them from all points, and then, as they trotted away, to note their action . . .

Until the Forest was fenced, lane-creepers were expressly excluded from the Non-Hand-Fed classes, and many were the disputes about which ponies were or were not to be put in this category! Today there is the similar but less contentious problem of deciding whether a pony has been hand-fed or not. If food is put out for some, there is no way of ensuring that *this* pony eats it and *that* one does not. But few if any that run on the Forest throughout the year are hand-fed in the generally accepted meaning of that term, and the class is usually more accurately delimited as Forest-fed. In the early days judging took place over about four days, but today it is likely to be spread over as many weeks. It often happens that an entered mare foals just before she is to be judged. This is unfortunate, as she will inevitably have lost some condition – more so than those due to foal later.

SUMMER ON THE FOREST

Mares have been known to foal in every month of the year, but the majority give birth in April, May and June, a time when the prudent commoner keeps a close watch on his animals. Comparatively few mares have difficulty in foaling, but a number of foals die each year. Some fall unseen into bogs and ditches, and die of starvation; some few are attacked and killed by foxes immediately after birth; others are rejected by their dams, though these can be hand-reared if found in time; far too many, inevitably, are killed on the roads; and a few are killed by stallions. The arrival of the foals heralds the most delightful time of the year. There can be few more enchanting sights than young foals playing together, bucking and galloping, and engaging in mock fights. Sometimes the foals play with their dams, and on occasions, as Stephanie Tyler has recorded in her study *The Behaviour and Social Organisation of the New Forest Ponies*, colt foals and yearlings play and play-fight with stallions – to the obvious concern of the youngsters' mothers, who stand by whickering and whinnying.

Although the stallions will generally indulge in gentle play with the youngsters, there are frequent encounters between rival adult males during the breeding season that are anything but gentle. Battle is usually joined when a strange stallion approaches another's herd of mares. Teeth and all four feet are used in a brief vicious struggle for supremacy. One minute the pair are up on their hind legs, 'eyeball to eyeball', striking fiercely with their forefeet, and the next they are down on their knees, each trying desperately to bite the other's head and neck. Sometimes the encounter ends in a brief running battle, during which the fighting pair may gallop blindly into walls, trees, or fences before the victor finally chases his opponent away.

During the early summer, too, the knowledgeable commoners are watching for the animals to shed their winter coats, as those that lose them quickly usually pick up condition better, Those that 'keep their hair on their backbone' are often poor doers and will need careful watching during the following winters. It is noticeable that some of the yearlings remain shaggy in patches right up until August, and have hardly shed their first winter coat before starting to grow the next.

Towards the end of April comes the first of the Beaulieu Road sales, although this one does not affect the ponies out on the Forest very much, as few of them are in sale condition. Mares heavy in foal or with young foals at foot are not accepted. Most of the animals entered are those that have wintered on the holdings; registered stock, halter-broken, partly broken or suitable for breaking; a few yearlings; a number of mares; some riding ponies; and possibly one or two stallions. The first sale of ponies on the Forest is usually held during the first week in August, when a number of mares with foals, and yearlings, are rounded up. This is followed by two sales in September, two in October and one in November. At the last five sales the bulk of the season's 'crop' of foals is sold, with colts outnumbering fillies by more than two to one.

THE ROUND-UP

The rounding up of the ponies for sale, and for tail marking and branding, is by far the most exciting and spectacular event in the New Forest, and has been compared time and again with scenes from the Wild West. There are undoubtedly many similarities, but the commoners impart their own particular flavour and some very special skills to a boisterous, hard-riding, sometimes callous, often unintentionally funny, and nearly always dangerous occupation. The main round-ups or 'pony drifts' are organised by the agisters, who advise the commoners of time and place, and any good rider is welcome to take part.

A number of permanent stout wooden pounds are strategically sited throughout the Forest, some in the narrow driftways between inclosures, where the ponies have few escape routes open to them. On the day of a drift a larger portable pound of wooden or metal sections is often erected next to the permanent structure, and animals can be driven into that also. As the time of the drift draws near, riders appear from all over the district and beyond, some in horse-boxes, some in trailers, a few from the more adventurous local trekking centres or riding schools, and others apparently from nowhere. The agister who is organising the drift collects the riders (anything up to twenty or so) and tells them the approximate whereabouts of the ponies to be drifted, how he wants them brought in and at what pace – Let's take them slowly' is the usual instruction, which is forgotten the instant the herd starts moving. He then stations walkers and cars to cut off any remaining escape routes, giving orders to these of his helpers to head the ponies off, almost on penalty of death! The riders then move off, leaving spectators to ponder over the motley collection of horses and ponies on which they are mounted. Some commoners swear by Forest ponies, especially stallions, which can twist, turn and accelerate with quite unbelievable speed, and are very sure-footed; others prefer half-breds, which are generally bigger and faster than Foresters, possibly give their riders more thrills, and certainly more spills, but tend to go lame more easily; and others again ride Arabs.

Once out on the open Forest the riders select a bunch of ponies and fan out behind and to each side to cut them off and drive them in. Then the fun starts. The wily old mares have an unerring instinct about groups of riders approaching them. Trekkers, casual riders, or riding schools can pass within inches of them and they won't bat an eyelid, but the moment the colt-hunters (as the riders are called) come into view, up go their heads and they are away, flat out across the rough heather or bracken-covered ground, which is often pitted with clay holes and rabbit warrens to add to the hazards of the chase. If there is any nearby cover, such as deep woodland and gorse brakes, they invariably head straight for that, where they can split up and be lost almost within seconds.

Casualties among the riders, of course, are quite common. On one well remembered occasion, described by Verderer Hugh Pasmore, one agister's pony turned a somersault over a hidden drain within minutes of starting a group of colts, a commoner's wife was shot off her stallion into a bog, another agister galloping after her horse came down and was kicked in the face, and a young lad was swept off his pony by a low branch – a grand total of four falls in an incident-packed twenty minutes. Fortunately for the survival of the commoners, such wholesale destruction is not normal. Sympathy for fallers is not overwhelming, and the following snatch of conversation between colt-hunters as they galloped side by side is from an impeccable source. 'Old George's on the floor back there – I think he's broken his leg'. 'Well – mark where he is and we'll go back when we've got this bunch in.'

The pace at which the ponies come in is often breathtaking. Out on the open heathland they can be specks on the horizon one minute and thundering into the pound the next. It is a noisy affair, with the riders shouting at the ponies and at each other, and the walkers waving their arms and yelling to head the ponies off from gaps in the woods and drive them into the pound. When one drive is finished, the colt-hunters stop briefly to give their dripping, heaving ponies a breather – then they are off again to hunt out the next bunch. During the course of a day four or five drives may bring in 100 or more animals. Some drives are more successful than others, and the post-mortem following a run that starts with a group of twenty mares and foals and ends up with one unwanted filly is something to be wondered at!

While the riders are out on the last drive of the day, some of the commoners light a fire beside the pound to heat the branding irons. As soon as the colt-hunters gallop in with the last bunch, the real business starts. On a given word, the commoners jump in among the ponies and, with more shouting and waving and brandishing of sticks, cut off a small bunch and drive them into a smaller enclosure in the larger pound, called the crush. The general idea is to keep mares and their foals together, but inevitably some are separated, and above all the other noise rises the agitated whinnying of dams calling youngsters and the shrill calls of foals shrieking for their mothers. Once in the crush, the agister moves quickly among the jostling excited animals, and skilfully cuts or 'marks' their tails with his particular mark, carefully keeping the cuttings of horse hair – traditional perks of the job. The marking of the tail shows that the owner has paid his fee for the year. How the agister avoids being kicked is something of a mystery, and says much for the temperament of the ponies, as only rarely does one lash out with any vicious intent. While the ponies are in the crush, a commoner stands by with a worming gun and doses those animals their owners wish to be treated.

Before long the branding irons are in use, on foals that are to be left on the Forest as replacement brood mares or on potential stallions. (Among themselves the commoners usually call all foals colts, referring to fillies as mare-colts, and colts as horse-colts.) Catching a colt, particularly one that has been born wild and free, is no easy task, even in the confined space of the pound, and it often takes three or four men to overpower the frightened struggling little animal. Then, with one man hanging grimly on to its tail and another at its head, it is pushed up against the fence and a patch of hair cut out on the near shoulder or saddle, ready for the brand. Someone runs to the fire, picks out the correct iron, and quickly applies it to the patch. There is a plume of smoke, a smell of burning hair – and the job is done so quickly that the foal does not realise it has happened. It certainly feels little, if any, pain.

Every pony on the Forest must bear its owner's brand, which is registered with the verderers and can thus be identified easily. Some of the brands are simple initials, but others are strange-looking hieroglyphics. The story is told of a minor panic caused by one of the latter during World War II, when an agitated old lady rang up the secretary of the pony society, then Sir Berkeley Pigott, and told him she was sure the Germans had landed in the Forest and were using the ponies – she had found an animal with a swastika brand on its shoulder. It certainly was a swastika brand, but it belonged to a commoner, who had used it for many years before Hitler appeared on the scene.

When the work of branding, marking, and worming is over, the gate at the far end of the crush is opened and the animals stream out. Some are taken away by their owners - those likely to winter badly perhaps, a stallion wanted as a riding pony, or maybe foals to be sent to the next sale.

COLT-HUNTING

As can be seen, pony drifting is a somewhat hit-or-miss affair, for every pony in a particular area does not necessarily come in, and those missed are not tail-marked and in all probability not paid for. The payment of marking fees has been likened to income tax in that some people seem to get away without paying, but it is impossible for the agisters to check every animal on the Forest. Drifting, too, does not take into account the needs of individual owners: for example, a mare and foal may be brought in on a drift in September before the foal is old enough to be separated from its dam, and sold. As a result, a variety of alternative means of catching ponies when they are needed has been developed over the years. The most usual is for a commoner to collect several of his friends and ride out to bring in the animals he wants. This is known as colt-hunting, as distinct from pony drifting, and is every bit as exciting and in some ways even more hazardous.

When the groups of ponies are sighted, the owner points out

the foals he wants brought in, and the chase is on. The riders usually work in pairs to cut out mare and foal from the bunch. As the ponies gallop away, twisting, turning, and propping, the riders come alongside and gradually edge in until one is close enough to lean over and grab the colt's tail, give it a quick practised twist, and bring the animal down. The rider then leaps off his pony, (which, if well trained, will immediately stop and probably graze) and sits on the colt's head. His partner, having caught the rider's pony, returns with it, plus a rope to put round the colt's neck, so that it can be tied to one of the riders' mounts and taken back to the trailer or pound. Alternatively, one rider grabs the colt's tail to slow it down, while the other slips a rope round its neck. Of course, things do not always go according to plan, and if a foal leaves its dam during the chase, it can prove much more difficult to catch. It has also been known for riders to 'bale out' catching a colt, only to see their mounts disappearing rapidly in the direction of home. Some commoners send well trained dogs in to dense woodland and scrub to search for groups of ponies and give tongue when they find them.

Another method, employed by at least one well known commoner, requires remarkable courage, skill, and split second timing. Instead of grabbing or 'tailing' the colt, he gallops right up alongside it until he can get one arm round its neck. Then, still travelling at a fair pace, he jumps off his pony and somehow manages not only to get both arms round the colt's neck and bring it down, but keeps his reins looped round his arm as well. Immediately the colt comes down, the commoner sits on its head, keeping well back to avoid being kicked. His companion then gets a rope round the foal's head, and it is brought in in the usual way. Not surprisingly, mishaps have occurred from time to time. Once, the rider managed to get his arms round the colt's neck, and leapt off his pony as usual, but in the effort he also leapt clean out of his Wellingtons, leaving them standing upright in the stirrups, while he thrashed around on the rough ground in his stockinged feet.

If there is a pound or a field nearby, colt-hunting becomes a scaled-down version of drifting. Small groups of mares and foals are driven in, the wanted ones caught up, and the rest turned out again.

There have, needless to say, been some legendary colt-hunts. One of these concerns the eventual capture of Mrs Parsons's Deeracres Winston Churchill, when he was only a few months old. He was running with his dam and her yearling foal near Brockenhurst. His dam was one of the really wild mares that had not been brought in for two years. A group of three of four commoners went after her, and she ran them for no less than two hours all round the outskirts of Brockenhurst before they managed to get all three ponies into the pound at Bridge Farm on the north-east side of the town. The colt then leapt out (no mean feat for a foal only a few months old) and ran for another half hour all round the back of Brockenhurst, until finally cornered in the pound at The Weirs, on the opposite side of the main road.

Perhaps the most famous story concerns the aptly named Mockbeggar Outlaw, who evaded capture for no less than eight years. Time after time the commoners went to catch him, and time after time he outwitted or outmanoeuvred them, or, although he only stood 12·3 hands, simply outran them. Finally an ultimatum was issued. If he was not brought in, he would be shot, as he was becoming too much of a nuisance. So a last determined effort was made. His owner Raymond Bennett, Raymond's wife Sheena, and a number of friends went out and soon found him in his usual haunt. Immediately Outlaw went into his well tried and successful routine of jinking, turning, and twisting, and as the riders galloped to cut him off, he turned at full gallop and raced off in the opposite direction. Eventually Mrs Bennett and a friend, both riding half-bred Foresters, managed to catch up with him near Janesmoor Pond on Fritham Aerodrome. They galloped side by side, with Outlaw between them going just as fast as they could, and finally managed to run him into Broomy Pound. Once in, he put up a desperate fight, clawing at the sides and trying to jump out, but the pound withstood his onslaught and the Outlaw was finally coralled. It was estimated that the little pony had run his pursuers at least 4 miles at a full gallop over all sorts and conditions of going before being caught.

Strangely enough, once having been brought in and then moved to another part of the Forest, he now comes in quite happily on the drifts nearly every year, and seems to be a reformed character.

Yet another means of catching up ponies, especially if they are going through woodland, is very occasionally used by some of the older commoners, who take advantage of the ponies' habit of walking in single file along well worn paths about 10yd apart. They set up ropes with a noose at one end on holly or other bushes at head height, with the loops over the paths and the fall or free ends attached to whippy branches so that the animals will not break their necks. Then the ponies are walked slowly through the wood until they are a short distance from the ropes, when they are sent on at a trot. If all proceeds according to plan, their heads go through the noose; as they feel the rope, the ponies instinctively pull one way or the other, thus tightening the noose and holding them firmly.

Occasionally on a warm summer's day, if the flies leave them in peace, the ponies stand or lie in the sun, dozing quietly. This gives the owner a rare opportunity of creeping quietly up and slipping a ring-rope round their necks and catching them without a long exhausting chase. But, as one commoner ruefully remarked: 'It's not as easy as it sounds. Either they're not asleep when you think they are, or they sense you're there at the very last minute – and they are away.'

One way or the other the ponies are caught, and some form of drifting or colt-hunting continues through September and October, ceasing only with the last of the sales in November. During this time the commoners keep an eye on their mares, because those that have had their foals taken away are likely to lose condition, until their milk dries up. Then, all being well, they should pick up again before the first of the hard weather comes along. No foal under the age of four months may be entered for sale, so those that are born too late in the season are either kept on the Forest for their first winter or taken in and kept on the holdings until the following spring.

7

THE MARKET FOR PONIES

THE WORKING PONY

For centuries the ponies have provided the commoners with at least a part of their livelihood, either from sales or as working animals on holdings. The market for livestock of any kind is always subject to fluctuations, but perhaps because of the breed's ability to adapt to changing conditions, the New Forest pony has nearly always been in demand. Before the general use of wheeled transport they found a ready market as pack and pannier animals, their sure-footedness, great strength for size, and general hardiness making them ideal for the job. Most of their work was doubtless legitimate, but in the 'good old days' of almost universal smuggling among country folk many a Forest pony found itself, hooves bound in sacking or leather to deaden the noise, being led up from the coast at Christchurch, Mudeford or Beaulieu with a couple of casks of contraband liquor slung across its back, or its panniers stuffed with fine silk or laces. Burley village was on one of the old free-trading routes from Mudeford, and in Pound Lane the ponies were tethered in the shelter of a huge drooping yew tree known as 'The Dockyard', while their cargoes were stowed safely away.

The introduction of wheeled vehicles provided the commoners with yet another use for their ponies, and it was as draught and harness animals that they were chiefly used until the early days of this century. With the coming of the Industrial Revolution and the ever-increasing demand for coal, the smaller breeds of native ponies were bought in their thousands for work down the pits.

70

Plate 13 Her Majesty the Queen with HRH Prince Andrew, driving Mrs E. H. Parsons' Deeracres Sally and Garth Remus at Windsor

Plate 14 Mrs C. M. Green's mare Priory Pink Petticoats, showing the style which won her the first Whitbread Trophy for the Performance Pony of the Year

Plate 15 The late
Mr Ted Burry and the
prolific prize-winning
mare, Dolly Grey IX

Plate 16 The famous
post-war foundation
stallion, Brookside
David

Plate 17 Brookside
David's equally famous
grandson, Mrs B. A.
Roberts' Peveril
Pickwick

Some of the smaller stockier Foresters went to the mines, but in general they were considered too large and lacking the necessary substance, and were much more commonly sold for use in tradesmens' vans, and as a working man's means of transport. (Some of the skewbald ponies still remaining in the forest, however, are almost certainly descendants of a few coloured Shetland ponies that were introduced in an unsuccessful attempt to breed more suitable animals for the mines.) The breed society in the first decades of this century encouraged the 'utility' use within the Forest by including classes at the annual show for ponies 'suitable for carrying a man to his work, the property of commoners, bona fide working men, occupying not more than 10 acres', as well as ride and drive classes.

As the industrial age progressed, and a new wealthy middle-class arose, so came the demand for the breedier type of Forester as a children's riding pony and for light harness work drawing traps and governess carts. This provided a welcome outlet for the lighter boned, lighter framed descendants of the Arab and TB crosses, which were so unsuited to life on the Forest, while the 'old fashioned' short-legged stocky ponies were still sold in appreciable numbers for draught work. Then came the motor car, and within a few years the market for harness animals collapsed. But for the efforts of the breed societies, the effect on the New Forest ponies could have been catastrophic. Fortunately for the commoners, the pony society publicised the breed in a variety of ways, and took sensible and effective steps to continue its improvement so that by the 1920s, with the revival of interest in riding as a sport rather than the sole means of transport, a steady and ever-increasing sale of riding ponies had begun. Since the end of World War II the remarkable increase in all types of equestrian pastimes, particularly the rapid rise in membership of the Pony Club and riding clubs, has created a market for ponies not only in the United Kingdom but throughout most of the Western world.

DEALING

The commoners have a centuries-old tradition of horse dealing, either privately or at local fairs or markets. A writer in 1906 remarked that there were two ways of selling Forest ponies – either as suckers at Martinstown Fair in Dorset in mid-November or at Ringwood Fair in December, or as yearlings at Lyndhurst Fair or Britford in the following August. Later still, organised auctions were held both at Brockenhurst and Lyndhurst, and when Brockenhurst market was closed, the auctioneers moved to a private sale yard opposite Beaulieu Road station, about 3 miles from Lyndhurst. However, at the beginning of World War II when foals went for the rock-bottom price of 5s per head, this was no longer economic, and the yard closed. Fortunately the pony society was in a position to step in, and having obtained the necessary permission, built a new yard on the present site at Beaulieu Road. Messrs Thos Ensor of Dorchester took over as auctioneers, and have conducted sales on behalf of the society ever since.

Going to Beaulieu Road is rather more than just going to another pony sale – it is an opportunity to observe a slice of traditional Forest life. The sales start at 10.30am, but from early morning the scene is one of great activity, with lorries, horse-boxes and trailers discharging their loads of ponies. As the lorry doors open, the ponies come out, uncertainly at first and then with a rush, and are herded into the pens by the sale ring. With the final indignity of a catalogue number stuck on their quarters, they stand more or less patiently and wait their turn for auction. The commoners and their families also wait, looking forward not only to seeing their animals knocked down for good prices but to one of the important 'days out' of the year.

Most of the crowd collect round the pens, leaning over or sitting on the rails, and the talk is naturally centred on the ponies – the quality of animals for sale, and whether prices will be up or down on last time. For the prospective buyer a little discreet eavesdropping could pay dividends. The commoners' ability to recognise individual animals, even foals, is well known, and an overheard remark – 'I see that old chestnut colt of Jackie's is here. That's by old so-and-so's horse. It could be a good one' – may be worth acting on. The sale ring itself is surprisingly small, and

74

seems smaller still when the crowds of buyers and spectators pack into the tiered stand as soon as bidding begins.

At 10.30 the door to the chute opens and the first foal comes in, perhaps erupting into the ring and rushing about in the confined space, threatening the safety of the stewards, who try and direct their wild charges with flags. At least one has been known to leap the fence, scatter the startled crowd, jump out of the yard and disappear into the depths of the Forest. Others enter hesitantly, and stand, forlorn and frightened, in the centre of the ring. But no matter what happens in the arena below him, the auctioneer launches into his patter: '*What* a lovely foal this is, and a filly too! Isn't that a well grown foal! What am I bid? Thirty guineas, thirty-five – and a half. Thank you, sir. It's against you, madam. Come along, he's only a man, don't let him beat you!' And so it goes on, hour after hour, until the last pen is empty, the last animal sold. Then comes the business of new owners loading their purchases into boxes, lorries or trailers – some going easily, some resisting violently. Many a lorry has left the sale yard with its sides reverberating from the sound of hooves (fortunately unshod) battering at the boards, or a trailer departed with a pony's head sticking out through the small gap between ramp and roof.

The majority of animals sold at Beaulieu Road go as children's riding ponies. A buyer with a real 'eye for a horse' might pick up a genuine bargain. Black Ribot, for example, was bought at a sale in 1959 for fifteen guineas. He was broken and schooled by the owner's daughter, Marilyn Jewell, who then took him show-jumping. He was upgraded to J A in one season, and by 1967 was valued at £1,500. Another bargain was Setley Ethel, the 1971 New Forest Young Stock champion at the Royal Show, who was bought by Mrs Frampton.

Allegations are still made that dozens of ponies are sold at Beaulieu Road for the meat trade. Certainly during the war years some were bought for human consumption and when prices are low enough (as in 1974), numbers of the plain bay colts still find their way into tins of pet food. Perhaps a quick humane death in a British slaughterhouse, however, might be preferable to a living death in the backyard of a totally ignorant, inexperienced owner who had bought an animal on impulse because it was cheap. Nevertheless, over the years, genuine concern has been voiced that Forest ponies were being bought by continental buyers for slaughter abroad, under conditions believed to be far less humane than those in this country. While it cannot be stated categorically that this has never happened, a certain amount of sleuthing has been done, and so far no proof has been forthcoming. In 1965 the council of the pony society asked for any evidence of such a trade, and the National Pony Society (NPS) offered a substantial reward; but nothing even remotely conclusive was produced. With transport costs at their present level, it does not seem an economic proposition for foreign buyers to deal in New Forest ponies which, for the most part, do not carry much meat.

From time to time there has been criticism of the conditions at Beaulieu Road and the handling of the ponies. In the early 1950s this reached a peak, with questions in the House of Commons and adverse publicity in the national press. The pony society was asked to submit a report to 'The Committee of Inquiry into the Slaughter of Horses' set up by the Ministry of Food. The report made it clear that the society received no financial benefit from the sales, and that the auctioneers customarily made a grant towards the upkeep of the yards. It went on:

The ponies from the time they arrive till they leave the saleyard are under the supervision of the police, officials of the RSPCA, eight stewards appointed by the Society, the Hon Secretary and the Hon Veterinary Surgeon. Only foals that have reached an age when they have been or should be weaned are sold; they are penned separately from the other ponies. The ponies are handled by local men with lifelong experience of unbroken ponies. No sticks are allowed, the ponies being controlled with flags. Hay and water is provided. Being public auction sales, it is impossible to state with any accuracy the ultimate destination of the ponies. These sales enjoy a very high reputation in the pony world, prospective purchasers coming from all over England and even as far afield as the lowlands of Scotland, to buy ponies as foundation stock or for their children. Allegations recently made in Parliament and elsewhere that the Society acts in collusion with the London butchers, that it breeds ponies to support the meat trade, and rounds up ponies on the Forest to assist the meat market are without foundation and are as unworthy as they are untrue.

In 1968 a complaint was made by a committee member of the NPS about the handling of ponies, and the vice-chairman of that society visited Beaulieu Road and reported his findings. These were not for general publication, but the New Forest society was given permission to publish them in the 1968 annual report. Without divulging any of the contents, it can be said that the report was entirely favourable and concluded that everything possible appeared to have been done to ensure the ponies' welfare.

Doubtless further criticism will be received in the future, for pony sales at best are emotive affairs. Only the most unimaginative can view the packed pens with complete equanimity, and not spare a thought as to the destination of these engaging animals, some of which, as recently as the previous day, had been enjoying the freedom of the open Forest.

Prices over the years have varied enormously. The annual report of the Burley and District Society for 1907 mentions yearlings being sold for £8 and suckers for £3 15s, but with an average for yearlings of between £4 and £5, and top prices of around £25 for Forest-bred harness ponies of 12·3 to 13 hands. The boom in the sale of all kinds of horses reached a peak in 1972–3, with prices at Beaulieu Road reaching £115 for yearling fillies eligible for registration, and a top average of £72, but by 1974 the picture had changed dramatically, owing to the increase in the price of fodder. Although the top average for eligible yearling fillies was £47, many colts went for under £10 – far from an economic price for commoners paying marking fees and transport costs, and supplying winter feeding.

EXPORTS

Since World War II an extremely healthy export trade in New Forest ponies has grown up. As long ago as 1909 enquiries were received from the USA, but interest waned when it was learned that no form of breed registration existed. However, in 1951 Mrs S. C. Deeds exported her four-year-old mare Nancy's Fancy (by Bettesthorne Caesar) to the United States, and in 1955 she sent Miss E. Tresilian's Beacon Perdita (bred by Miss Macnair), which as a three-year-old had won her class at the National Pony Show. In 1956 Miss L. M. Brown exported Brockwell Sue's Moonlight (ex Minstead Sue) to Mrs Carroll Wilson of Massachusetts. Miss Wood of Rockbridge, Ohio, imported the two-year-old colt Deeracres Sir Anthony (by Goodenough ex Deeracres Pierrette) in 1957, and also Mudeford Diana III, which subsequently produced a fine colt foal by Brookside David. The writer Monica Dickens bought Virginia from Mrs D. Stephens; and four riding ponies, including Beechern Nanette, went to Mr John B. Bayer of Connecticut. In 1960 Mr Carmichael of Cleveland, Ohio, came to the Forest and bought Deeracres Hurricane (by Knightwood Spitfire out of Queen Bee) and Garth Carlo (by Newtown Dandy ex Garth Charmer) to take back for his children to ride; both ponies went extremely well for their young owners, and Hurricane was a big winner in jumping and hunter-pony classes.

By 1957 the overseas market had expanded to include Canada, Holland, Denmark, Sweden, Norway, and Luxembourg, and in due course exports increased to a record 525 in 1972. As home prices have declined since then, and costs increased, the export trade has dropped off – partly no doubt because overseas countries are breeding their own stock, and partly because of the statutory minimum prices placed on all ponies exported from the UK. This was done with the idea of keeping the export price well above the continental meat-trade price, but, as with much arbitrary legislation, there are anomalies. For instance, the minimum rates depend on height – £160 for a Forester of 12 hands or over and £120 for one under 12 hands. Shetlands, on the other hand, are in a special category and may be exported for half that price, in spite of the fact that there is probably more meat on an adult 10-hand Shetland than on a 12-hand Forest foal. Thus the Shetlands could conceivably go for meat, whereas the Forest foal probably would not – which is fine for the Forester.

Perhaps not seriously counting as abroad is Lundy Island, in the

Bristol Channel, though the sea crossing can be rough enough. In 1928 the island's owner, Martin Coles Harman, bought a number of mares and fillies at Beaulieu Road, and two stallions (one a TB) to take there. The sea trip must have been quite an experience for them, and on arrival they had to swim from boat to shore. The foals of the TB were, not surprisingly, found unsuitable for the rugged winter conditions on Lundy, and various other stallions, including Welsh and Connemara, were used. The predominant colour of the Lundy ponies is dun, and in 1972, with the idea of going back to the original type of Forest stallion and keeping the dun colour, the island authorities leased Mr Bessant's premium stallion Greenwood Mistrel.

The first Forester to be exported to Australia was the four-year-old Burton Sligo, in 1909, but the next batch of registered ponies did not get there until 1970, when they were greeted with considerable enthusiasm. Temperament, size, good bone, and the ability to carry a rider from childhood to adulthood are among the attributes that appeal to Australian breeders, and already an increasing number of organisations are providing special classes for Foresters in Australian shows. Some allow the larger animals up to 14·2 to compete in open classes, as the height limit for ponies in Australia is 14 hands. The Australian Pony Stud Book Society has made provision for a New Forest section in its official Stud Book, and in 1973 the New Forest Pony Society of Australia was formed. Within a year it had members in Victoria, Queensland, New South Wales, and South Australia, and interest is growing all the time. Plans are in hand to produce in four generations Australian New Forest ponies using the British New Forest standard as a guide. These ponies are to be placed in 'Section B', and will be distinct from animals registered in the UK Stud Book, which will come under 'Section A'. A 'Section C' register will provide for other mares, geldings and entries of not less than 50 per cent New Forest ancestry. Provision is being made for official inspection of first-cross females at two years old, and only stock of a suitable standard will be admitted to the 'C' register.

One of the first imports was a member of Mrs Green's famous 'Priory' line – the stallion Priory Sunshade – bought on the

79

advice of R. S. Summerhayes by Miss Passlow of the Sumerae Stud, Booloumba, Queensland. (The stud is named in honour of Mr Summerhayes.) Miss Passlow also bought Marley Fantasia, who is now leased to Mrs Nita Appleton of Wattle Ridge, Gippsland, Victoria. Mrs Appleton also owns Fantasia's first colt foal (by Sunshade) – Sumerae Sun Fantasy. The next emigrant was Broadlands Bright Seraphin, imported by Mr and Mrs Brian Charlton of the Erinskay Stud, Peterson, NSW, and Mr and Mrs David Blackburn of the Pahake Stud, Panton Hills in Victoria. In 1971 Mrs Max Barkla, wife of the Australian society's publicity officer, imported the grey stallion Mudeford Peter Piper (by Mudeford Pete ex Hucklesbrook Cha Cha and bred by Mr A. E. Burry), and the mare Sway Surprise Mist of Marley, who was in foal to Mrs Robert's Peveril Pickwick, and soon afterwards produced the colt foal Kalya What the Dickens. She later had two filly foals called Kalya Miss Pete (registered UK and Australia) and Kalya Clear Sky, both by Mudeford Peter Piper. Sadly 'Misty' died from an unknown cause three weeks after the birth of her last foal, which is being hand-reared and has been entered in the open foal class at the South Australian International Expo pony show. Before her untimely death, Misty won the brood mare championship at the South Australian Light Horse Breeders' Association show, and two similar awards at the Pony Breeders' and Fanciers' Association of South Australia. Kalya What the Dickens is already over 14 hands, and has been broken most successfully to saddle. At the time of writing he has sired two filly foals, one out of a part-bred Arab and the other out of an unregistered Welsh mare. His promise as a sire of galloways is attracting attention.

Canada also has a thriving population of Foresters, which are registered with the Canadian Pony Society and the Canadian National Livestock Records. The first pony to be imported was Mudeford Grey Streak (by A. E. Burry's Brookside David ex Mudeford Grey Gem); he was sold as a five-year-old to Ralph Mist, who stood him at stud in the UK, where he sired a number of good ponies, including the premium stallion Corra Tanty. When Mr Mist left for Canada, he took Streak and a cross-bred mare with him, and there sold the stallion to Dr and Mrs John Holbrook of Dundas. Ontario. The pony settled in remarkably well, and proved to be, as Mrs Holbrook writes, 'a fantastic performer, attending Pony Club meets with his child rider, being champion pony at Junior Shows, a member of the winning team at the 1961 Pony Club Rally, and hunting with the Hamilton Hunt'. He was also shown in Working Pony, Pony Jumper and In-hand classes in which he won championships, reserve championships and best of breed, and was champion stallion at the Pony Breeders' Show every year he was shown. He was second in the Cross Country Individual Standing, and even took part in a Pony Club display dressed as a clown. In other words, he was kind, generous and versatile – a typical Forester.

In 1960 the Holbrooks came to Britain looking for potential brood mares, and bought four: Mopley Danette (by Denny ex Gusty by Leygreen Sandy), who was in foal to Oakley Jonathan, from the Hon Mrs Rhys of Burley; Merrie Mitzine (by Duikers Prodigal Son ex White Moth) and Fleck (ex Minstead Victress) from the Sibleys' stud at Corhampton; and Oakley Pink (ex Dark Pearl) from C. Purse of Burley. These were the foundation of the Holbrooks' Forest Hill New Forest Stud, where Streak was the foundation stallion. One of his progeny was Mopley Maid (ex Mopley Danette), who was reserve champion hunter-pony over fences and reserve all breeds at the Canadian Pony Breeders' show in 1972, and is owned by the Sweeny family of Cincinatti, Ohio.

In 1968 the Holbrooks again visited the UK, to replace Streak, who was then twenty-two, and chose Miss Anne McGrath's Vernon's Starling (by Burton Starlight ex Melita). They also bought Merrie Mittens as a potential brood mare. Vernon's Starling took over from Streak in 1970, and has, to quote Mrs Holbrook again,

... become the star and darling of the New Forest in Canada. He has distinguished himself not only as boss of the herd, but in performance under tack as well. He has 16 youngsters, all good looking, lovely disposition, really fine ponies to show for himself– and has been champion stallion for 4 successive years at the CPB show, and to add to his glory he has won the New Forest pony under saddle two years running, ridden by a lady. I also have him broken to drive in harness.

The grand old man of Canadian Foresters, Mudeford Grey Streak, began to fail early in 1975 and was put down at the age of twenty-eight, having carried on the splendid tradition of the Brookside David line across the Atlantic.

Mr and Mrs George Huck of Goderich, Ontario, were so impressed by the Forest Hill ponies that they decided to start a stud of Foresters themselves. Mr Huck visited the UK and bought the winning two-year-old stallion Merrie Mars from the Sibleys, with Merrie Maundy to accompany him. The stallion sired a champion filly foal out of Merrie Starlet (by Mudeford Grey Streak).

Although the Forest Hill stud has produced some 50 ponies in all, the breed has spread less quickly than might have been expected. One of the reasons for this is almost certainly the cost of importing foundation stock from Britain. Mrs Holbrook gives a telling example. In 1960 they imported four mares, at a total outlay of $1,500 (including the purchase price); and in 1970 they bought two mares, but the shipping costs alone were $2,000. That, unfortunately, speaks for itself.

Europe has always been the largest market for Forest ponies. Exports to Denmark, chiefly of riding ponies, began in the late 1950s, but in 1960 a special order was received for two matching black geldings trained to harness for the golden coach in the Tivoli Gardens in Copenhagen. Mr Ron Ings located two black stallions, and in spite of the fact that one was four and the other five years old, and they had never been handled, broke them to harness. After only two months they went to their new country, where they settled into a way of life vastly different to that they had left such a short time before.

In the early 1960s the Danes became interested in breeding Forest ponies, and quickly established a stud book and a sub-committee of the Danish Pony Breeding Society for the breed. A strict and comprehensive system of grading ponies has been devised to ensure that only the best are accepted as breeding stock. The mares are graded in the autumn, when the owners bring them to various meeting places for individual judging. The judges give a description of each animal, which is included with the grade in the stud book when the pony is accepted for full registration; after its initial grading a pony may be brought before the judges twice more to try and improve its grade. Judging is very thorough, with each point of the pony being considered carefully, as well as its action and type; but English judges who know this method, and agree that it is much more painstaking than just 'lining them up', make the point that quality and presence, being indefinable, are sometimes ignored. There are three grades – best of breed or top quality, second best, and satisfactory but no more. Stallions are graded in the spring, and those not making the second best grade at the second attempt are rejected. All mares must have registered parents and grandparents, and stallions must have three generations registered. In addition, certificates that they are suitable for riding and breeding must be countersigned by the New Forest Society secretary.

With such a large pony population it is difficult to pick out individual animals, but of the stallions, one of the most successful is Beacon Pericles (by Denny Danny ex Bettesthorne Kate), bred by Miss Dionis Macnair and exported in 1962. Pericles has sired good ponies that have, in a number of cases, reached top grading. Deeracres Mayking (by Goodenough ex Edithmay), bred by Mrs Parsons and a big winner before being exported in 1963, has also sired good stock. One of the leading home-bred stallions is Yksi (by Musical Box ex Deeracres Golden Gorse).

In 1957–8 the stallion Wigley Nomad and twenty-one mares were exported to Holland, where they were introduced to large and enthusiastic crowds at several major shows. So impressed were the Dutch by the versatility, perfect temperaments and general appearance of the ponies that by 1960 they had imported well over 100, had formed their own breed society (headed by Mrs de Laitte Nanninga) and started a stud book. They have become the largest single overseas market for Foresters (in 1964 460 were exported from Britain), importing some very fine animals including Mr Sibley's Merrie Mistral (by Denny Danny), the late Mr Burry's David Gray and Mudeford Grey Ranger, Mrs Harvey-Richards's Knightwood Palomino, and F. C. Bennett's Setley Pride (by Goodenough ex Setley Poppet), which was exported as a two-year-old. Mares bearing prefixes that in themselves are almost a guarantee of quality include Mudeford Princess (by Brookside David ex Mudeford White Star), Mudeford Star (also by Brookside David), Weirs Queenies' Pride (bred by Mr Burt), Priory Nuts and May (bred by Mrs Eyre), and others too numerous to mention.

Sweden entered the market in the 1950s, importing the stallion Bettesthorne Hector (by Newtown Spark out of Bettesthorne Jessica) and nine mares in 1957, and Mr Burry's yearling colt Mudeford Brown David in 1963. Others included Deeracres Summertime and Mudeford Peter, and they were joined by Luckington High Star and Oakley David. Burton Starlight was exported to Sweden in 1970, and in 1972 a record total of 150 ponies went to various destinations in that country.

In 1966 an article by Nils Ljunggren reprinted in the British pony society's annual report praised the temperament and character of the ponies, and outlined the rigorous standards of judging at Swedish shows and the controls exercised over the conformation and general suitability of all stallions allowed to stand. Mr Ljunggren was highly critical of the general run of stallions he saw in Britain, and also of the English style of judging compared with the Swedish, in which the judges are obliged to give a commentary on each animal – a requirement that would surely decimate the judges' panel if introduced at English shows! He suggested that, if the Swedish way of judging was not soon introduced into England, Swedish breeding stock will be better than English. In defence of the English system, let us say that English judges who have visited Sweden are concerned that breeding of Foresters there appears to favour the 'horsey' type, with a consequent decrease of bone and substance, and increase in height and legginess. Inevitably this leads to the elimination of the indefinable 'pony' characteristics. But this problem is not only found in Sweden; it is a seemingly inescapable consequence of striving for the marketable extra size.

A big boost was given to exports to Germany in 1970, when the society arranged an exhibition at the Catherston Stud, Brockenhurst, for a party from the Kiel Pony Society – resulting in the sale of over thirty ponies. The exhibition included an in-hand class for ponies of two years old and over, excluding stallions and brood mares; a schooling display; ridden registered mares and geldings four years and upwards; a parade of first-cross ponies by TB or Arab out of registered mares; a driving demonstration; an exhibition of mounted games by the Pony Club; a parade of ponies for sale, and a jumping class for registered ponies. The visitors were also shown some of the Forest, and visited a few local studs. A similar type of exhibition was held again in 1972.

After a comparatively late start in the 1960s, many Foresters have been exported to France, notably by Mrs Harvey-Richards, and there are now few countries in the Western World where at least a small number of the breed cannot be found. Perhaps the most exotic destination of all was Nepal, where one Forester was sent in 1961.

8

THE ADAPTABLE FORESTER

A GENUINE FAMILY PONY

We have claimed that the Forester is the ideal family pony, capable of taking part in a wide variety of activities, and there can be few better examples than Beelzebub of Ramblers, owned by Mrs Nancy Keymer of Burley. Bubbles (as he is affectionately known) is by the great Brookside David out of a Forest mare, and was bought as a four-year-old for Mrs Keymer's daughter, who rode him in all the usual Pony Club activities, and later took him on to riding club events. Ridden by Mrs Keymer's son, he twice won the children's race in the annual Boxing Day point-to-point over a mile and a half of open Forest, and in 1972, when ridden by Mrs Keymer herself, he won the special award for the highest placed New Forest pony in the Ladies' Open Race over a distance of 3 miles. He has also been broken to harness. When he was a seven-year-old, Bubbles was introduced to polo by Mrs Keymer's son Edward; and the pair became so successful that they were picked for the local team, which came second in the finals of the national Pony Club's tournament at Windsor. During that year they also played at Cowdray, Rhinefield and Kirklington, which in itself must be a record for a Forest pony. Having mastered the game of polo, with its special requirements of quick turns, rapid acceleration and all-round manouevrability, Bubbles then applied these talents to gymkhana events, at which, not surprisingly, he was brilliant. The same speed and handiness made him ideal for colt-hunting, a pastime he regarded as the greatest fun. He viewed the confines of the show-ring with something less than enthusiasm, but nevertheless won show classes, as well as working pony and working hunter, and was in the show-jumping team for competitions between the New Forest and Holland on several occasions.

When her daughter married, Mrs Keymer took Bubbles over as her hunter. He is now in his ninth season with the Buckhounds, and has also been out with the South Dorset, the Wilton and the Devon and Somerset Staghounds – going equally well over these widely differing countries. Following hounds is his great joy in life, and he takes a six hour day in his stride. If Mrs Keymer boxes him to a meet and then has to come home early or finds that the day is cancelled, she finds it almost impossible to get him back in the trailer! He also knows when his owner is dressed for hunting, and enters the trailer with no trouble at all on these occasions.

In 1972 Mrs Keymer decided to enter Bubbles for the Golden Horseshoe Long Distance Ride from Salisbury Racecourse. In his Pony Club days he had taken part in the Rufus Stirrup ride in the Forest, and later he had competed in the pony society rides. Pony and rider qualified for the Golden Horseshoe in May when they were both fit from hunting, and then Bubbles was kept up through the summer until the final in September, instead of being turned out. Mrs Keymer entered with no more than a determination to finish the course – 50 miles on the first day and a further 25 on the second – but at the end of the first day she was astonished to find that they were averaging 8·8mph, and were thus in line for a Silver Horseshoe award. They set out on the second day, having passed all the veterinary checks with flying colours, and went beautifully until the last steep hill, where they were forced to slow down and drop their average speed; but they finished with full veterinary marks, and qualified for a Bronze Horseshoe – Bubbles being the first native pony to do so. (This achievment was topped in the 1975 Golden Horseshoe Ride by Mrs Cordall's Nigger Step gelding Bridgelea Starlight, who is the first native pony to win a Golden Horseshoe.)

Bubbles is now fourteen, and still thoroughly enjoys his day's hunting and an occasional chukka of polo. He acts as escort on Pony Club rides and picnics, and is lent to children taking their C and D Pony club tests – he reached B standard with the Keymers. So, be it hunting, jumping, showing, driving, colt-hunting, gymkhanas, polo, or long-distance riding, Bubbles will tackle it with zest, and, what is more, with considerable success; and it matters not a whit to him whether he is being ridden by Mrs Keymer, her son or her daughter. In other words, he is a true family pony.

NEW FOREST SCOUTS

It seems a far cry from a family pony to a member of a mounted infantry troop, and with all their merits, New Forest ponies do not automatically spring to mind when one thinks of ideal mounts for the Army. The very qualities of toughness, courage, strength, and adaptability that characterises the breed today, however, led to the formation in 1899 of the New Forest Scouts, a mounted company of the 4th Battalion of the Hampshire Volunteers. A contemporary account recorded the preliminaries:

> The black week in December, 1899 [start of the Boer War] . . . was also the immediate cause of the birth of the Scouts. When, in answer to the Government appeal for volunteers who could ride and shoot, the first contingent of the Imperial Yeomanry was raised, it suggested itself to certain well-known gentlemen of the New Forest that in their district was an ideal recruiting ground for exactly that type of mounted troops which seemed to be most required. A conversation in the train between Lord Arthur Cecil – the well-known authority on pony breeding – and Hon John Scott-Montague – the Member for the New Forest Division, set the ball rolling . . . A company of mounted infantry recruited entirely from the Forest and mounted on Forest ponies, took part in the annual training of the Hampshire Volunteer Infantry Brigade at Swanage in August, 1900.

The ponies were nearly all the property of the troops themselves and had spent most of the year running on the Forest; so they were considered particularly suitable for the rigours of war. The riders were of all weights and sizes, but the training sessions of a minimum of 30 miles a day carrying a man and his equipment, including a heavy army saddle, left the ponies relatively unscathed. Lord Lucas wrote in 1906:

We have a breed unsurpassed in hardiness and endurance. To know this you do not need to have seen the horses in the New Forest Scouts at the end of a 50 mile day in camp last year, when many of the bigger horses were lying down dead beat and refusing their feed, whilst the Foresters – some of them only 3 year olds, stood up and emptied their nosebags, not one of them being sick or sorry.

They were considered ideal for service in South Africa, and were recommended for a grant from the War Office; but it is not known how many, if any, actually went. Lord Arthur Cecil, one of the prime movers in forming the Scouts, certainly went, and returned with two Basuto ponies and a zebra. The latter he put to a Forest mare, which subsequently produced a dun filly with chocolate stripes!

The Scouts took part in activities other than training, and in 1902 they entered a team for the Auxiliary Forces jumping competition and won it. The team consisted of a 14-hand first-cross Forester and a 13·3 pure Forester whose rider weighed 12 stone and stood 6ft. At the same tournament another member of the Scouts won the Sword v Lance competition.

In spite of the Scouts' enormous popularity (there was a waiting list to join), Government support was eventually withdrawn, and they were disbanded. By then, however, they had demonstrated yet another of the Foresters' talents.

IN HARNESS

The ponies have always gone exceptionally well in harness. The commoners used them in their 'trucks' for haulage on the holdings and up to the 1930s, when they were ousted by cars, they were popular for private driving turn-outs. Interest in driving as a show class revived after World War II, but Welsh Mountain or Hackney ponies, with their rather more showy action, often had the edge over Foresters in this specialised field. Nevertheless Chocolate Soldier, bought at Beaulieu Road for only a few pounds by Mrs Glenda Spooner, and subsequently owned and driven by Miss Spacey, was virtually unbeatable in private driving classes in the immediate post-war years.

A famous pair of 12·2 Foresters, Garth Remus and Deeracres Sally, owned and driven by Mrs E. H. Parsons, gave the lie to the belief that the breed could not produce spectacular movers. In the 1960s they swept all before them in driving classes, their successes including first at the Royal International and first and reserve champions at Richmond. In 1962 Mrs Parsons was asked by Col (now Sir John) Miller, the Crown Equerry, if she would consider letting the pair go to Windsor for a season, for Her Majesty the Queen to drive. Mrs Parsons was delighted to agree, and spent some time introducing the ponies to the beautiful harness and vehicle sent down to her. During their stay at Windsor, Remus and Sally were driven by Her Majesty, Prince Charles and Princess Anne, before returning to the Forest to be shown again in private driving classes. At the time of writing both ponies are still going strong at twenty-one years of age; Remus has just retired and Sally has been a brood mare for some years.

Abroad, too, New Forest ponies have been used in harness. A Master of Hounds in the USA recently drove a Forest stallion to a sleigh when exercising hounds in the snow.

With membership of the British Driving Society growing, and with it the popularity of driving as a pastime (as distinct from competition), Foresters are being used more and more. Their sensible generous natures make them ideal for the job and, most important, they are safe in traffic.

Before tractors and lorries took over the moving of timber in the Forest, the Forestry Commission drivers often used to hitch a pony as lead to their teams of heavy timber-hauling horses to guide them out through the woods. What a sight it must have been – a diminutive Forester leading a team of huge Shires hauling great logs with nothing but the driver's voice to guide them as they threaded their way through the trees!

THE SHOW-RING

The potential of New Forest ponies as circus performers has never been seriously explored (fortunately, some would say), but a letter in the pony society's annual report for 1957 from

Mrs de Laitte Nanninga in Holland suggests that, with training, they could more than hold their own. Shortly after the arrival in Holland of the second group of Foresters from Britain, an invitation was received inviting them to take part in a demonstration at a big indoor jumping show. Mrs. de Laitte Nanninga takes up the story:

> This, of course, was a great chance to show the Dutch people what can be done with a New Forest pony. To get ready for the show, we had only about 5 weeks for training both children and ponies. The mare Brown Sugar, a 7 year old, was chosen as the pony for the Voltige (vaulting) group. At first she did not at all like it if one of the children landed too far back, and her hind legs would fly up in the air! But with daily training she soon got used to the work. The youngest child in this group was 7, and the oldest 14. By the end of the training, the eldest children could stand on the pony's back while she cantered around.
>
> Setley Rising, a very placid 2 year old filly, was trained at Liberty. This was done practically entirely by 2 boys, after they had been shown the way by a grown-up expert. She was taught to waltz, jump through hoops, kneel, lie dead, and jump up and stand on a bale of straw. Merrie May was trained to go in harness, and after only 2 weeks was trotting round with her show-trap as if she had never done anything else. Her driver was a boy of 16. Minstead Surprise and Charity were ridden in an 'A la Fleche' number – Surprise with a boy in the saddle and Charity trotting along on long reins in front. The different movements were made at the walk and trot only, as the time was too short to attempt them at the canter. Lastly 3 ponies were ridden under saddle in a simple programme of dressage. One of these, Mudeford Kitty, had shown herself such an easy jumper, that a boy was quickly trained to show the jumping possibilities of the New Forest ponies.

This remarkable demonstration becomes even more extraordinary when one learns that Minstead Surprise was only halter-broken when she arrived, and that *all* the foregoing activities took place in the arena *at the same time*. As R. S. Summerhayes remarked in an article in *Riding*, '*What* an advertisement for the breed!'

POLO

Mrs Keymer's Beelzebub of Ramblers made a name for himself

in Pony Club polo, but he was just one of a long line of polo-playing Foresters. In 1946 and 1947 some members of the Rhine-field Polo Club (in the Forest) played on Forest ponies, and in 1947 they made a small piece of polo history by sending a team containing a Forester to the County Polo Association's tourna-ment at Roehampton. The pony in question was Shobley Hazel, a 13·1 hand-mare by Minstead Hazel, owned and ridden by Sir Berkeley Pigott. She moved the polo correspondent of *The Times* to write, 'Rhinefield started with a fast run initiated by Sir Berkeley Pigott on a diminutive but game and fast Forest pony . . . Kennard and Pigott, whose little pony sustained a severe tackle, made it 2–4 between them'. Sir Berkeley himself, writing in the pony society report of 1953, commented that she '. . . was willing to try to ride off anyone. She has given many a beginner their first taste of polo and appears to enjoy every minute of it, always bucking when she first goes on the ground'. Hazel was a tremendous character in many ways. She was quite accustomed to being transported by trailer, but preferred to travel with her back to the engine and her head hanging out of the rear. Her obsession with speed in and out of the trailer resulted in her being fitted with hobbles when travelling to save the vehicle from being bat-tered to pieces.

RACING

Speed and endurance, particularly over rough going have always been features of New Forest ponies, but until 1911 this had mostly been exploited in colt-hunting. In 1911, however, the Burley Pony Society accepted an idea from committee member R. Roope-Reeve to hold a point-to-point flat race across the open Forest on Boxing Day. The following were the main conditions governing this first historic race:

> The competitors will ride from the starting point to the winning point by any line they like, there being no flags on the course or other restrictions as to the line to be taken.
> The meeting place will be made known where competitors are to assemble, but no competitors will be told the starting or finishing points until the day of the race at the meeting place, so that it will

not be possible for anyone to go over the course before the race.

The meeting place will be announced to competitors and be published on the Society's Notice Boards and elsewhere as the Committee determines.

The owners of ponies entered must be members of the Society.

Ponies entered must be registered New Forest ponies.

There will be a handicap of weight for inches; the minimum weight to be 11 stone for ponies up to 13 hands, and thereafter 7 pounds for each inch.

All ponies will be measured immediately before the race, and no allowance will be made for shoes.

Competitors must weigh out immediately before the race on on the weighing machine (kindly provided by Mr S. Wright) and weigh out immediately after. They must provide their own weights.

No spurs are to be used.

Twelve competitors lined up for the start near Millersford Bridge in pouring rain, with the going as deep as it could be and very rough in places. The finishing post was at Ocknell Pond, 3½ miles away. According to the official account, the race was run at a great speed and there were four falls. Duster (ridden by by J. Street) and Purewell Rufus (J. Dear) came down in the deep ground near Puckpits; and The Nun (Lord Lucas) inexplicably fell on good going, bringing down Burton Bluebell (E. Burry). In spite of falling, The Nun, a 13·2½-hand pony carrying 12st 7lb came in first – an appropriate and popular win for the president of the society – and the experiment was voted a great success all round.

The point-to-point was not the only race the Foresters ran that year, but the other, against a team of Dartmoor ponies, ended on a decidedly sour note, as the extract below from the Burley and District New Forest Pony Society 1911 Annual Report makes clear. A team of four Forest ponies (The Nun, ridden by Lord Lucas; Purewell Bay Ronald, owned by G. Lander and ridden by R. Reeve; Burton Bluebell, owned by W. Burry and ridden by E. Burry; and Carmelite, P. S. Kershaw) travelled down to compete at Huccaby Races over a 2½-mile course across the moor.

This race, which was intended to be a sporting test of the respective merits of the New Forest and Dartmoor breeds of ponies, proved to be an unfortunate experiment in every way. The Dart-moor team included some ponies which could not be proved to have any Dartmoor blood in them at all. In addition to this, the measuring of the ponies and the weigh-in was conducted in a very unfair manner. In these circumstances, as could only be expected, the New Forest team was easily beaten. It is greatly to be regretted that a challenge of this kind should have been taken up in so unsportsmanlike a spirit!

Needless to say, that experiment was not repeated, but the Boxing Day point-to-point has continued, with modifications and additions (except for seven years during and immediately after World War II) until the present day, to become one of the great features of Forest life. Over the years the number of races has increased until now there is a full card of seven, including two for children over a mile and a half, and from time to time there have been special races for veterans and colt-hunters, and open races for non-Forest ponies or horses. It is almost certainly the only true British point-to-point left, requiring great skill, endurance and an intimate knowledge of the Forest in picking the quickest and best way between two points, and avoiding the intervening bogs, ditches, clay holes, low branches, and assorted hazards that the Forest can present in infinite variety. Falls are common and often spectacular. One young rider in the children's race of 1958 took a header into a mud pool – both pony and jockey emerging unscathed but looking like something out of the Black and White Minstrels' show. Immediately they finished the rider's mother dumped him straight into the nearest pond, though it is probably not true that she broke the ice in so doing.

As the choice of route is left to the riders, it has been known for finishers to come at the winning post from opposite directions. On several never-to-be-forgotten occasions riders have lost their way and come in ten minutes or so later than the winner, the judges mistaking them for the first home in the next race before noticing that their ponies were the wrong size! To prevent such confusion, riders in different races now wear different coloured numbers.

The veterans' race has provided some remarkable finishes. Ted Burry, who came second to Lord Lucas in the first race in 1911, won it three times, and only gave up after a very bad fall when he was well over seventy. In 1966 the runner-up to Mr Burry was Mr A. Whitehorn, who was eighty! In 1971 Mr and Mrs Cree, riding Miss Mohawk and Salome respectively, provided a delightful touch by crossing the finishing line hand in hand. Another well known couple finished a race (not the veterans') less auspiciously, colliding as they reached the post and one of them falling off.

The children's race is nearly always packed with incident, as the youngsters usually have even less control of their excited mounts than the adults. On one marvellous occasion they started their 1½-mile journey in a real 'cavalry charge', only to arrive back at the start some short time later, having described a complete circle!

Another incident that caused a certain amount of chaos occurred when a rider found he was under weight at the very last minute, so he stuffed his pockets with carrots. Unfortunately he weighed out light at the finish, having laid a trail across the Forest as the carrots bounced out of his pockets. Rumours that it was done to distract the other ponies were firmly denied!

DRESSAGE

At the other end of the equestrian scale from the gay abandon of racing is the highly disciplined art of dressage – and once again a New Forest pony has performed with distinction. Robin (by Forest horse ex The Lady) was owned by Mrs P. Seaton Stedham, who bought him as a stallion at Beaulieu Road. He was only about 13 hands, and had been put up for sale because of his habit of jumping into neighbouring fields and gardens; within the first five minutes of arriving at his new home he showed his disapproval by jumping out over his 4ft 6in stable door. After being gelded, he was schooled, and in 1949 made his debut in dressage – coming fourth at Portbury in a contest in which he was the only pony, and finishing only a little behind Conquistador, the champion dressage horse of 1951. At Camberley he came fourth again, and in the Dressage Championships at Henley he came third in the Novice and fifth in the Medium, again being the only native pony competing. In 1950 he won and was placed several times in open competitions, reaching his greatest heights when coming second to Mrs V. D. S. Williams's Clogheen at Camberley and fourth in the Dressage Championships.

In the slightly less exalted but nonetheless exacting Prix Caprilli competition Miss Susan Bailey's Mockbeggar Smokey was a member of the Ringwood and District Riding Club team that won the Area competition at Tidworth to qualify for the National Riding Clubs' championships at the National Equestrian Centre in 1971. The team finished fourth.

There seems no end to the variety of tasks Foresters can and do perform willingly and with distinction. Their abilities as colt-hunters have been proved beyond question in the Forest, and they have also shown their worth in the rather less hectic annual cattle-drives. Official recognition of their suitability as stock ponies has recently come from Australia, where Mrs Nita Appleton's Sumerae Sun Fantasy has just been accepted for the Appendix of the Australian Stock Horse Stud Book. This is a particularly fine achievement, as animals under 14·2 hands are only accepted if they are exceptionally good – and 'Fanny' is 14·1½ hands. Finally, at home, a Forester in the North of England has recently been awarded a prize as a shepherd's pony.

9

IMPROVING THE BREED

As has been shown, the early attempts to improve New Forest ponies by the introduction of Arab, TB, and carthorse blood were not an unqualified success, and had these unsuitable out-crosses been allowed to continue, the future of the breed must have been in jeopardy. Equally, however, some form of improvement was necessary, as by the late nineteenth century the ponies were considered by some to be in real danger of extermination by constant in-breeding. Fortunately for the ponies a number of perceptive people living in and near the New Forest recognised the danger and did something about it.

BREEDING INNOVATIONS

The beginning of the ponies' salvation came with the forming, on 10 February 1891, of the first of the breed societies – the Association for the Improvement of the Breed of New Forest Ponies. Encouraged by the verderers and guided by outstanding personalities such as Lord Arthur Cecil and Lord Lucas, the association set about encouraging the commoners to retain their best colts, to be turned out later as stallions, by a system of premiums and prizes – later supplemented by premiums donated by the Board of Agriculture. The society also organised an annual Stallion Show at Lyndhurst, during which the verderers inspected and passed the stallions to run on the forest, and the various prizes were awarded.

We have previously mentioned Lord Arthur Cecil's introduction of stallions from other native breeds and Lord Lucas's

97

introduction of Welsh ponies of the Dyoll Starlight strain, as well as an excellent bay which combined the blood of Hermit with an Exmoor strain. On cross-breeding Lord Arthur wrote in *The Field* of 1910: 'The best cross is either the Welsh or the Exmoor, and there is a very large proportion of Highland blood in them now which gives substance and constitution without size.'

The commoners, however, suspicious as always of outside interference, were initially less than enthusiastic. They maintained that it was useless to turn out good ponies, since there were bad ones still on the Forest; but by about 1910 current informed opinion was that the type of young stock showed that the best stallions were more than holding their own. A report from *Country Life* in that year made the point entertainingly:

> A beautiful little Welsh pony turned out by Lord Lucas had established itself in the Forest and rounded up a nice herd of mares. Presently there appeared one of the pests of the Forest, the sort of coarse, common pony not quite bad enough to be excluded, and about half as big again as the little Welshman. With his ears laid back and neighing out threats and defiance, the intruder galloped up, expecting an easy victory over his small antagonist. But matters turned out quite differently. Rare courage and power, derived from a long line of hardy ancestors, were packed into the Welshman's small frame. Without a moment's hesitation, he made straight for the big pony, knocked him clean off his legs, and planted two or three resounding kicks on his prostrate antagonist, who, scrambling to his feet, made off in the direction from which he had come, hotly pursued by the gallant little Welshman.

That the introduction of outside pony blood was considered a success is made clear by a report on the 1911 stallion show submitted by the judge, the Rev T. F. Dale, a noted authority on mountain and moorland ponies in general and Foresters in particular:

> Not only were the ponies better than in past years, but they were well shown . . . The plan of infusing fresh blood into the New Forest ponies by turning out onto the Forest stallions of kindred and some hardy races seems to result in more bone, some increase in size, and to diminish the faults of the native breed . . . It has been

said that the number of stallions from other parts of the country turned out in the Forest has practically left the Forest ponies without a type . . . but coming fresh from riding over the Forest and visiting the mares and foals in their especial haunts, I am struck, but not surprised, to observe how the New Forest types still prevail.

In 1912 the Board of Agriculture offered six further premiums of £5 each for stallions, subject to a number of conditions designed to ensure that the right type of animal was selected. The Board stipulated that the ponies must belong to one of the recognised mountain and moorland breeds and that they must be typical of the breed it was desired to perpetuate; the premiums would be paid after the service season, provided agisters could certify that the ponies had roamed at large from 5 May to 1 August in one of half dozen selected districts of the Forest.

The Improvement Association also experimented in controlled breeding with the object of maintaining the true type of Forest pony. For example, in 1935 the champion stallion at the show, Orchard Pershore, was turned out in the old Polo Field at Brockenhurst, and members of the Association were permitted to turn out registered mares with him at a charge of 2s per week. Classes for foals by the stallion were included in the stallion show for 1936 and four special premiums of £2 each were awarded to yearling colts in 1937. In that year the stallion chosen was Jason Weller, and five of his colt foals were awarded £5 premiums at the Burley Society's show.

REGISTER AND STUD BOOK

The Improvement Association continued to do sterling work, but it is probably true to say that it came to be somewhat overshadowed by the Burley and District New Forest Pony and Cattle Society, founded in 1906. This society was in no way set up as a rival to the Improvement Association, but to be complementary to it – as the first president, Lord Lucas, was at some pains to point out to the verderers when he asked for their approval of its plans. Its founders had for some time realised that the improvement of stallions was of prime importance, but no matter how good they were, the breed as a whole would not benefit to the

99

full unless steps were taken to improve the quality of the mares as well. So the new society had as its objectives (1) to compile a register of New Forest ponies belonging to members of the society, (2) to encourage the preservation of the best breeding strains by giving premiums to mares, and by other means, (3) to endeavour to obtain winter keep for the ponies of members, and (4) to take any other measures necessary to promote the general interest of the breeders of New Forest ponies and cattle and the stock they bred.

The compilation of a register was considered to be a matter of urgency, not only as a means of establishing the whereabouts of the ponies and their ownership, but for enhancing the reputation of the breed and widening the potential market by being able to prove to prospective buyers that an animal claimed as a Forester was genuine. It would also make judging at the Society's show much easier, for hitherto practically any pony's owner could claim it was eligible for the New Forest classes, and disputes were not unknown. In compiling the Register the society sought the verderers' permission for the agisters to send the names of all the animals marked on the Forest to the secretary, who would then register them and allocate a number to each. For the purposes of registration a pony must have been known by the agisters as a Forest pony; its dam must have run on the Forest for at least one season as a three-year-old and upwards; and its sire must have been passed at Lyndhurst or by the verderers, or be standing in the New Forest Parliamentary district. These conditions in themselves give some idea of the knowledge the agisters were expected to have of the animals in their districts. But even they were not required to know every pony, and a further condition required that if the agisters were unable personally to recommend registration, the owners were expected to bring sufficient evidence to satisfy the committee that their ponies were eligible.

From compiling a register it was a short and logical step to embarking on a proper stud book, and proposals for this were put forward in 1909. The first volume was published in 1910, at 1s 6d to members and 2s 6d to non-members. It contained the pedigrees of all ponies registered up to 30 June 1910 (118 stallions,

356 mares, 49 geldings), and consisted of four sections: stallions
of four years old and upwards passed at Lyndhurst (by the verderers) during the previous three years; New Forest stallions
registered under the rules of the society and those standing at
stud in the New Forest Parliamentary district; New Forest pony
mares; and a supplement for geldings. In addition to the usual
details contained in stud books, such as the names of the owner
and breeder, description, breeding, produce etc, information was
given about the district in which the pony ran, and special types
were cut so that every owner's brand could be shown. The
Improvement Association cooperated in this very important
venture by supplying full particulars of the stallions receiving
premiums at the Lyndhurst show. In his introduction to Volume 1
the Rev T. F. Dale wrote about the uses and importance of a
stud book as follows:

> ... it may be hoped that such a book will enable us to trace the lines
> from which to develop ponies for riding, driving and draught ... A
> Stud Book carefully used is a source not only of instruction but of
> pecuniary profit to the breeder. For by the greater opportunity
> which it gives him to select mares of the right type, he is enabled
> without additional expense to improve the quality of his stock
> and thus increase his profit. I have visited sales of pony stock in
> many parts of England and I have always been struck by the readi-
> ness of buyers to pay somewhat higher prices for stock of better
> quality. And here again a Stud Book is an advantage to the breed,
> for it puts buyers into possession of the information most useful
> to them, in finding out the best ponies to buy. .... Moreover the
> book soon reveals to us the success or failure of experiments in
> breeding. It may be said that where stallions are turned out to run
> on the Forest, pedigrees must always be a matter of guess-work.
> But the history of Exmoor shows us that this is not so ... I believe,
> and have always advocated the theory that without a Stud Book
> no breed can hold its proper place in the estimation of home and
> foreign buyers. And I believe – and for this belief the New Forest
> owners themselves have given me the opportunity of laying the
> foundation – that with the establishment of the New Forest Stud
> Book, a new era of fame and prosperity will begin for the breeders
> of this invaluable stock.

Volume 2 of the stud book was published in 1912, but from

1914 until 1959 arrangements were made to include the New Forest registrations in the stud book of the National Pony Society, once each registration had been approved by a local registration committee. Not until 1960, some 32 years after the amalgamation of the two older Forest societies into the present New Forest Pony Breeding and Cattle Society, was a separate stud book once again published, largely due to the efforts of the then secretary, Mrs E. H. Parsons.

PREFIXES AND AFFIXES

The use of prefixes had been common among pony owners for many years. For instance, Lord Lucas's ponies were usually prefixed by 'Picket', G. Lander's by 'Purewell', V. Pinhorn's by 'Bickton', and J. and G. Bramble's by 'Avon'. In 1946 the pony society introduced an official register giving members the exclusive right to a particular prefix or affix, subject to the approval of the council. In 1961 it was also decided that, when an owner had not bred the pony he or she was registering, the prefix would be added to the name and become an affix. This was to avoid confusion, and still allow the breeder's own prefix to be used before the name. Since the register came into being, the use of prefixes and affixes has become widespread, and some of the most famous of recent years include 'Mudeford' (A. E. Burry), 'Brookside' (the Misses Jackson, then Miss O. Golby), 'Beacon' (Miss D. Macnair), 'Beechwood' (Hon Mrs Rhys), 'Deeracres' (Mrs E. H. Parsons), Priory' (Mrs C. M. Green), 'Peveril' (Mrs P. B. Haycock), 'Knightwood' (Mrs Harvey-Richards) and 'Tomatin' (Mrs R. Taylor).

BURLEY SOCIETY SHOWS

The breed shows organised by the Burley Society at Burley Manor Park were impressive annual events, and a glance through the old programmes confirms that the policy of awarding premiums was carried out. Conditions to ensure, as far as possible, the retention of the best stock on the Forest were attached to most of the awards.

There were a number of other conditions, including one that

the fillies should run on the Forest for at least four months every year. But one of the most interesting points was the limitation on height. In 1913 one of the agisters had suggested that the limit of 13 hands for mares in show classes penalised the owner who did his ponies well, so that they grew over height; but his proposal that animals up to 13·2 be admitted was rejected at that time, although later the rules were revised. This was only one of a series of arguments, which have continued to the present day, about ponies much over 13 hands rarely doing well on the Forest. Indeed, in 1908, Lord Lucas wrote: '. . . we may safely take 13 hands as the limit of size that can be bred advantageously on the Forest, and as the standard towards which we should aim in our breeding . . .' But as the demand for riding ponies has increased, so have the pressures to allow the breeding of bigger animals. All kinds of compromises were suggested, and at one time there was the absurd situation that ponies in riding classes could not exceed 13·1 but children's hunters could be up to 14·2! The official height limit was then put back to 14 hands, before finally being fixed at the present 14·2.

Some idea of the versatility of the ponies even in the early days of the century, when the variety of equestrian activities was rather less than at the present time, is given by the range of classes limited to Foresters. Apart from the ordinary show classes, there were races, harness classes, ride and drive, jumping and one or two gymkhana events. The plan for the show-jumping course for 1906 gives an insight into the standard expected – remarkably high for ponies in an era when jumping was anything but the highly competitive and technical sport it is today. There were five obstacles – a bushed back hurdle, a 3ft 6in gate, 3ft 3in in-and-out hurdles with 14ft between them, a 3ft 3in wall and 10ft of water. A feature of the 1909 show was a race between Lord Arthur Cecil and Mr Reeks, both riding Foresters, which was won by a bare length by Lord Arthur.

NEW FOREST PONY BREEDING AND CATTLE SOCIETY

In spite of the deaths of Lord Arthur Cecil in 1913 and of Lord

Lucas on active service in 1916, the Burley Society continued to flourish, very much along the lines which have been described. In 1923 both the Burley Society and the Improvement Association suffered a loss in the death of the Rev T. F. Dale, who, in consultation with Lord Arthur and Lord Lucas, had been instrumental in initiating the stud book and the scheme for non-hand-fed mares on the Forest. His work as a judge and as a prolific writer in praise of the ponies did much to spread their popularity far beyond the confines of the Forest.

Interest in the Improvement Association, however, was declining, and when the honorary secretary, T. Stovold, resigned in 1937 because of ill health, with the probability of being replaced by Sir Berkeley Pigott, who was also honorary secretary of the Burley Society, the advantages of amalgamation became overwhelming. Thus, in 1938, the new Forest Pony Breeding and Cattle Society came into being, with the Hon Mrs Pleydell-Bouverie as president, Sir George Meyrick, Bt, as chairman, Sir Berkeley Pigott, Bt, as secretary, and Captain C. B. Lyon as treasurer.

The aims of the new society were similar to, but not identical with, those of the previous ones: they included registration of ponies in the New Forest section of the National Pony Society stud book; encouraging the preservation of the best type and breeding strains of ponies; allowing cattle of suitable type, and pigs, to run on the Forest; holding two annual shows, one in the spring for registered New Forest stallions, and the other on August Bank Holiday to encourage the improvement of registered ponies; and taking any other measures to promote the general interest of breeders. The society defined New Forest ponies in its rules: 'A New Forest pony is one already registered in the stud book or one known to the agisters as such or one whose dam was a registered pony mare who has run on the Forest for at least one season as a 3-year-old or upwards and whose sire was a pony stallion passed at Lyndhurst or by the verderers.' A sire of a New Forest pony was defined as 'a pony stallion not exceeding 14·2 in height whose name appears in the New Forest stud book or which has been passed by the verderers to run on the Forest, or by the council of this society'. These rules, which were no more then a redefining of those applicable when registration first began in 1910, were expressly aimed at preventing 'New Forest ponies, bred outside the Forest, in what might be called artificial sur-roundings, from being eligible for registration, as they would, after two or three generations, have lost the stamina which is the foundation of all mountain and moorland breeds.' (Many com-moners today wish that this rule still applied, so that they would not have to compete with stud-bred ponies!)

During its first year the new society made one or two innova-tions: it agreed to pay half the transport cost of approved local entries to the National Pony Society's show at Islington, in an an effort to advertise the breed (the half share of the costs for thirteen entries was £3 8s 5d), and managed to obtain an additional £34 for premiums at the stallion show, with the direct result of an increase of twenty-five entries and a far higher standard. This last step was considered necessary because the ownership of stallions had passed from the large Avon valley farmers to those who had little or no accommodation for them during the winter, and it was clear that sufficient financial inducement would have to be offered to owners to keep and maintain their best colts during the winter months, if there was not to be a shortage of good stallions.

It says a great deal for 'pony people' that in spite of shortages, restrictions and the general upheaval, the work of the society went on throughout World War II. Various activities had to be curtailed – for instance, in 1940 no field was available for the stallion-in-hand scheme because so many had been laid up for hay, and owing to transport difficulties the entries for the 1941 stallion show were the lowest on record. The non-hand-fed class was discontinued, and the advent of the blitz on the Monday before the first Beaulieu Road sale of 1941 prevented many buyers from the North and Midlands arriving. Soon after the outbreak of war the verderers issued an appeal to all pony owners to take in all those ponies haunting the villages and main roads, as it was feared that if such a pony was the cause of an accident to anyone en-gaged in war service, sterner measures might be enforced by the government. In order to prevent small commoners with in-sufficient land for these ponies having to sell their good brood mares and young stock, the society, together with the Commoner's Defence Association, advertised in the local papers for owners of keep who would be willing to take in these animals. By this means twenty ponies were offered free keep, and many owners also took the opportunity to sell off their lane-creepers. True to form, a few owners did not bother to remove any ponies, so that casualties on the roads trebled.

Considerable areas of the Forest were taken over by the Services, particularly the RAF, thus reducing the area available for grazing, and, as we have mentioned, certain areas were ploughed and sown. All this was strictly illegal, but under the circumstances the verderers felt they could not prevent it, though they never actually gave consent. One good thing did emerge from this wartime occupation. At the end of the war the verderers found themselves in a healthy financial position, owing to the comparatively large sums they had been paid in compensation, and they were able to increase the number of agisters from two to four.

Meanwhile the pony society, released to some extent from wartime restrictions, began to expand its activities. One of the first steps was the reintroduction of the non-hand-fed class, a popular move that resulted in an entry of sixty-six mares in 1946, compared with thirty-three in 1939. The judges, Mrs E. H. Parsons and Sir George Meyrick, commented on the great improvement in quality and condition that had taken place during the war years. Grants, first from the Racecourse Betting Control Board, and then from the Horse & Pony Benefit Society, enabled the scheme to continue unchanged until 1964, the year in which the fencing and gridding of the forest was completed. As all ponies were then confined within the perambulations, it was no longer possible to differentiate between lane-creepers (who had not been eligible) and mares who genuinely stayed on the Forest. In addition, it was society policy to encourage the feeding of hay in winter, and consequently the class was renamed 'Forest-fed', with the following conditions of entry:

A mare must be registered New Forest, be 5 years old or over, must have had at least 1 foal, must be in foal at time of entry, and must have run on the Forest continuously since she was a yearling, provided this last condition shall be deemed to have been fulfilled in the case of a mare that is known to have run on the Forest continuously from the date of the completion of the fencing of the perambulation to 1 March 1966 and has continued to run on the Forest thereafter.

In 1969 it was decided to offer £2 stallion premiums to animals that had wintered on the Forest and had not been to the stallion show, to cover the cost of catching them and having them vetted.

The stallion-in-hand controlled breeding scheme had also lapsed, and efforts to revive it in 1946 failed through lack of a suitable field. However, this was remedied for the 1947 season, when 21 acres were rented at Vereley and Mr Peckham's champion stallion Newtown Spark was turned out. Twenty permits to run mares with him were granted, but the society was disappointed that only two came from small commoners, who were offered free keep for six weeks for their mares and would have been expected to benefit considerably. As an added incentive, special premiums were offered at the 1948 August show for filly and colt foals by Newtown Spark, and subsequently for colts at the stallion show, until they ran on the Forest as three-year-olds. In 1948 Newtown Spark was again chosen, but in 1949 it was decided to turn out Miss E. F. Jackson's Brookside Spitfire, initially for a trial period of one month following the stallion show, as some doubt had been expressed about his capabilities as a stallion on the Forest in 1947 and 1948. On 31 May the committee heard conflicting reports and decided to ask Mr Peckham to bring back Newtown Spark and turn him out in the fields south of the drive. Spitfire was put in the fields on the north of the drive with the four mares he was known to have served, whereupon he lived up to his name, and, having negotiated two iron rail fences, savagely attacked his rival, Spark – for which lapse he was banished to the Forest for the rest of the season.

In spite of what might be described as a few local difficulties, controlled breeding continued, and it says much for the judgement of the committee that most of the animals chosen – for example, Denny Danny, Oakley Jonathan, Goodenough and Newtown

Spark – have gone down in breed history as great stallions, whose names appear in many of the pedigrees of the biggest prizewinners both at home and overseas. However, by 1959 the difficulties of obtaining suitable land had become overwhelming, and the committee also felt that, with so many private studs, the champion stallion would do more good running on the Forest – so the scheme was finally dropped.

From its inception at Lyndhurst towards the end of the last century the annual stallion show has always been of particular significance. The selection and passing of stallions to run on the Forest, which is vitally important, was done in the early days entirely by the verderers, though they probably consulted the Improvement Association, as they consult the pony society today. No selection procedure is ever without its critics, and a local press report of 1911 commented that there:

> ... was a little feeling because the Verderers did not pass several ponies which were docked, complaint being made that no notice was given of their intention not to pass such ponies. As a matter of fact, several years ago, the Verderers drew attention to the fact that ponies were brought to be passed with short tails, and to make things right now, the Verderers should give notice that they would not pass any ponies foaled in 1909 and docked.

The show continued to be held at Lyndhurst in the spring, with the accent on stallions running out on the Forest, but in 1956 private studs gained some acceptance by the institution of classes for stallions three years old and upwards who were kept in hand and not running on the Forest. This gave an opportunity for owners without Forest rights, or those who could not run their mares on the Forest for some other reason, to choose a good stallion. That this class was won by Miss Olive Burry's David Gray, with Mr Bennett's Goodenough second, and Mr Sibley's Merrie Mistral third, is proof enough that the standard was exceptionally high. In 1957 the ground at Lyndhurst was no longer available, so a move was made to New Park, Brockenhurst. At this show it was decided to reintroduce the ruling that no premium would be paid until the stallions had run on the Forest as three-year-olds, since many of the better colts were being sold as riding ponies after they had collected their two-year-old premium – a problem that remains with the society (in a slightly different form) to this day, and not only in connection with stallions. In 1960 a class for ridden stallions was introduced, and the annual report for the year commented on the exceptional manners shown by all entries.

For the next few years the show moved to Sway, then to Heathfield farm at Holmsley. In 1968 there were two shows, one as usual in the spring and a second on the Saturday of the August Bank Holiday weekend. The idea was that it was unfair for stallions that had been out all the winter to have to compete early in spring with animals that had been stabled until the day before the show; in August all would start more or less equal – and so it proved. There was also another, more humane reason behind the experiment. When the show was held only in the spring, some owners used to take their stallions off the Forest during the winter and feed them up so they would look their best. As a result, immediately after the show a large number of extremely fit horses were turned out on the Forest just at the very time when the mares, having had to fend for themselves throughout the winter, would not only be at their weakest but also heavy in foal. The stallions 'ran' the mares, which was probably the cause of many slipped foals, and the level of road accidents reached an intolerable pitch. Under the present system, with the majority of stallions being out either all or most of the year, there is much less commotion and upset. Criticism of this arrangement has come from people who believe that it is important for the stallions to be at their fittest during the service season.

The quality of stallions passed to run on the Forest has, from time to time, come in for unfavourable comment, and the pony society has always been conscious of the need to improve the standard. In 1969 a stallion working party was set up to consider the type of stallions to recommend the verderers to pass. It was agreed that the order of priorities in assessing a stallion to run on the Forest should be (1) fertility, (2) hardiness (ability to live on the Forest through the winter), (3) masculinity, (4) progeny, (5) conformation, (6) action, (7) colour and (8) pedigree. Height was not considered important, but it was recommended that the pony's history should be assessed in conjunction with every other point. The working party thought that conformation should be considered in the following order of priority: (1) good front, (2) good hocks, (3) adequate bone, (4) smaller heads, (5) good feet and straight limbs, and (6) reasonably high-set tails. Though of paramount importance, feet and limbs were usually good in the breed, and so, although care was recommended to keep them good, they were not considered top priority.

It was decided to recommend dividing the grant money (from the Racecourse Betting Control Board) equally – half to be awarded as premiums at the show for conformation and action, and the other half to be awarded to ponies on the Forest. All stallions which were in possession of a veterinary certificate, had been passed by the verderers, and which ran on the Forest, would automatically become eligible. The stallions would be judged in March and April on the Forest for hardiness, and those not out in the winter would lose hardiness marks (how many would depend on their history). Progeny would be looked at in July.

The recommended allocation of judging marks was as follows: hardiness 100; fertility and masculinity 50 each; and conformation, action, colour and pedigree 20 each. Fertility, although of top priority, was not allocated top marks, because it was felt that any horse suspected of low fertility should be tested, and removed if he failed the test. The ponies' history should be considered throughout. Marks for pedigree would be allotted as follows: eight great-grandparents 20; four grandparents 15; two parents 10; dam only 5; plus twenty bonus marks to be awarded at the discretion of the judges. The idea behind these recommendations was to encourage a pony that could really live on the Forest and produce useful foals, and the verderers were recommended not to pass stallions getting very low marks. The judges would be two selected by the pony society's council (at least one from the judges' panel) and one verderer.

These recommendations had scarcely been formulated before a highly critical report was received from the NPS inspectors of the standard and presentation at the stallion show of 1970, and they insisted that less money be paid to ponies on the Forest than to those at the show. As a result, the following additions and modifications were made to the scheme that had been prepared.

1. Premiums would be awarded to colt foals running on the Forest, which would be judged in July, when the judges would take the breeding of the foals into consideration and see the dams. Premiums would not be paid until the colt had run out as a four-year-old (half to be paid at four and the rest later), but ponies carrying premiums, if offered for sale, would be marked in the sale catalogue so that other commoners would have the chance to buy them. Premiums would approximately cover the cost of keeping a colt through his first winter, and, if the pony did not come up to expectations, would be paid in the same way as outstanding premiums are paid to colts that die before qualifying to claim them.

2. Fewer but larger premiums would be offered. The marks for judging stallions on the Forest would be revised as follows:

Conformation and action	130
Progeny	100
Hardiness	100
Masculinity	50
Fertility	50
Pedigree	20
	450

As previously, the pony's history would be considered throughout.

These recommendations were put into operation in 1971. Only six premiums were awarded in each district for the Forest judging out of a total of eighty-three entries, whereas at the stallion show twenty-two premiums were available to an entry of forty ponies.

The verderers' inspection takes place in the spring (the stallions that go to the show are passed there for the following year), and any not passed at the previous stallion show must be turned out before 1 May. They are judged on the Forest on how they have wintered, their conformation, movement, and masculinity, and then judged again in July on their progeny and fertility. In theory, judging fertility is impossible but, in practice, the judges, who know the ponies well, have a very good idea, and even if there are two stallions running in close proximity, they can usually distinguish the two sets of foals. It will also be obvious if a stallion has collected and held a reasonable bunch of mares, and whether a good proportion of them have foaled. In these instances the judges depend a great deal on the agister, who is also able to tell them if there have been strangles in the district or an abnormal number of slipped foals, and whether any other unusual circumstance has affected the number of foals, and hence their estimate of the stallion's fertility.

The mechanics of selecting and passing colts and stallions is quite complicated, and, as with everything to do with animals, a certain amount of controversy exists. All potential stallions have to be vetted when they are rising two, and certified as free from hereditary unsoundness and of reasonable conformation and physique. In addition to the standards of freedom from hereditary unsoundness required for a Ministry of Agriculture stallion licence, they must be free from sublaxation of the patella, and from parrot mouth or other malformation of the jaws. They must be passed every year until they are 5, but after that they are only inspected if a complaint is received or if they have not been running out continuously.

Each year about 120 stallions are passed to run out – and here controversy arises. Some say that 120 is too many for about 3,000 mares, although the 120 include some two-year-old colts, and that a sufficiently high standard cannot be maintained. The NPS report tends to support this view, but the commoners are dependent on the arrival of foals, and if sufficient stallions are not passed, all the mares may not be covered. There is then a risk that some commoners will take a chance and turn out unpassed animals. In the immediate past there has been a shortage of suitable colts presented, since their owners were gelding them and selling them for high prices as riding ponies. In such a situation, if a below-average animal is presented – particularly if he is the only one that will run in a certain district – it is almost impossible not to pass him.

Once passed, the premium stallions are allotted to their districts, where, in theory at least, they should stay for four years. However, if a stallion will not haunt in the district allotted to him, there is little that can be done about it, and he will be left to run in the district of his choice. There are also non-premium stallions, which, although passed by the verderers, can be turned out wherever their owner chooses, and they may chase off the premium animals, thus upsetting the allocation of districts once again.

Stallions passed to run on the Forest are exempt from Ministry of Agriculture licences, but all private stud stallions (which do not run on the Forest) have to be licensed at two years old. Some members of the pony society believe that for a breed with a height limit a life certificate issued at the age of two is inadequate, and have proposed that all stud owners should be asked to supply Joint Measurement certificates showing that their stallions do not exceed 14·2 hands at six years old. No problems of excess height normally exist among stallions on the Forest, however. A great deal of hard work has been put into devising the best means of improving the standard of stallions, and at last this seems to be showing real results: for the first time, in 1974, the judges were of the opinion that the stallions were of a higher standard than the mares.

In addition to its strenuous efforts to improve the breed, the New Forest Pony Breeding and Cattle Society has done a very great deal towards encouraging the widespread popularity of the ponies, and in holding events within the Forest to demonstrate their versatility. In 1958, with the idea of increasing the breed representation in mountain and moorland classes at shows outside the Forest, the society offered attractive rosettes for the best New Forest exhibit at a number of shows, and the scheme has proved so popular that in 1974 no fewer than sixty-two were awarded, with Mr and Mrs Roberts' outstanding stallion, Peveril Pickwick, gaining ten. Another innovation came in 1966, when a 30-mile ride round the Forest for registered ponies was introduced, with commemorative rosettes for finishers. Forty-two started and forty-two finished at an average of 5½mph; most finished well ahead of schedule, apparently because some veterans of the point-to-point thought this was yet another race, and went flat out for the first half mile! This event was held annually until 1969, when it was cancelled owing to a lack of entries, possibly caused by growing interest in the Golden Horseshoe Rides and preparation for the official qualifiers for this event.

Pony races were a feature of the Burley show from the early years of this century but from 1967 they have been held separately, latterly at New Park, Brockenhurst, in July, when they have attracted a large crowd.

In 1969 there was an opportunity to bring some of the best New Forest ponies to the attention of a very wide public, when the society was invited to take part in an exhibition of mountain and moorland ponies at the Royal International Horse Show at Wembley. Each breed was allowed to show four ponies, including a stallion and a mare and foal, and the pony society decided that, to enable a greater number of owners to participate, there should be a change of ponies half-way through the week. The following ponies were chosen: Mr and Mrs Sibley's Merrie Musket; Miss Macnair's Beacon Celia, with foal by Oakley Jonathan; Mrs Rhys's Randalls Leading Lady (riding pony); Mrs Parsons's Setley Springtime (harness); Mr Crabb's Burton Starlight; Mr Burt's Weirs Queenie's Good Luck and her foal by Howen Marshall; and Mr Kitcher's Silverlea Aries (riding pony).

In 1973 the New Forest Ponies of the Year awards, devised by Mrs Harvey Richards and Mrs Grayson, were introduced. The Whitbread Performance Pony of the Year award (sponsored by Messrs Whitbread Breweries Ltd) for the pony gaining most points under saddle, and the Ensor In-Hand Pony of the Year award (sponsored by Thos Ensor & Son of Dorchester and Otton's of Cranborne), are designed to promote interest in the breed, and to encourage owners to show their ponies over a wide area in a variety of events. The In-hand award is self-explanatory, but the Performance award is based on points gained in a wide range of events, from driving to racing and from dressage to handy hunter classes. First winner of the Performance award was, most appropriately, Mrs Green's lovely mare, Priory Pink Petticoats. The 1975 champion was Chris Beale's versatile stallion, Frank of Crabbswood (by Setley Springtime ex Pussyfoot). The first In-hand award went to Mrs Cave-Brown-Cave's Burton Honey's Delight (by Burton Starlight ex Burton Honey), and the winner in 1974 was Mr and Mrs Roberts's Peveril Pickwick.

Since the present society's formation in 1938 it has been especially fortunate in its secretaries. There have been just three in the thirty-seven years of the society's life, and they have all given generously of their time and extensive knowledge. The first was Sir Berkeley Pigott, who had the arduous task of guiding the new society through its formative years, including the difficult wartime period. He did much to publicise the breed, by speaking and writing about it, and by demonstrating its suitability as a polo pony. His contribution over the years in so many ways has been enormous. When Sir Berkeley retired in 1955, his post was taken by Mrs E. H. Parsons. She did much of the work in re-establishing a separate stud book and, with her Deeracres ponies such as Winston Churchill and Mayking, a great deal to stimulate interest in the breed in this country and abroad. Her famous pair of driving ponies, Sally and Remus, showed just what heights Foresters could attain in harness.

In 1966 the present secretary, Miss Dionis Macnair, took over from Mrs Parsons. In addition to the vast amount of work she puts into the society, Miss Macnair and her Beacon ponies are well known wherever the breed exists. Beacon Briar, Beacon Cressida, Beacon Pericles, to name but a few, have made their name at home and overseas, and the grand old mare Bettesthorne Kate not only won many prizes in the show-ring, but produced a string of winning sons and daughters by such illustrious sires as Denny Danny, Newtown Spark, Goodenough, and Knightwood Spitfire. As well as showing, judging, helping with Riding for the Disabled and taking part in society activities such as the point-to-point, Miss Macnair also became a verderer in 1974 – only the second woman to be elected to that position.

10

THE BREED TODAY

With the formation of the breed societies, the establishment of a stud book, and the influence of such eminent people as Lord Arthur Cecil, Lord Lucas, Mr Dale, and Miss Blackmore, it was not long before a number of local people took up pony breeding as a hobby. The pioneers I have just mentioned were very much concerned with elimination of faults introduced by indescriminate out-breeding, and they may be said to have laid the foundations on which the present breed has been built.

BROOKSIDE STRAIN

Probably the most prominent of the post-World War I era of hobby breeders were the Misses Winifred and Edith Jackson, who were joined by Miss Olga Golby in 1922. Together they bred the illustrious Brookside ponies; this prefix appears in countless winners' pedigrees both in this country and abroad. Most famous of their stock were the stallions Brookside David, Brookside Spitfire and Brookside Firelight. In the years between the wars they showed their ponies at local shows, but, of more importance to the breed as a whole, they took them up to the National Pony Society's show at the Agricultural Hall in Islington, London, where they were seen by a very wide audience. Miss Golby has vivid memories of travelling up in 'The Horsebox Train' to Waterloo station, where the ponies had to be persuaded to step down on to the platform, for there were no ramps then. The imagination boggles at the thought of the reactions of a stallion straight off the Forest to all the bustle and commotion of a busy railway terminal.

Once unloaded, the ponies had to be walked right across London to the show at Islington! Even allowing for the difference in the volume of traffic in those days, it says a great deal for the temperament of the ponies and the skill of the handlers that no more serious accident than the occasional slip-up ever occurred. The Misses Jackson had some notable successes at the show, including a first in 1937 with Brookside Judy, who went on to win the *Country Life* Challenge Cup for the best mountain and moorland in the show, and a second with Tommy Tucker. In 1940 the positions were reversed, with the stallion taking first place.

Quite a number of the Jackson ponies traced their ancestry back to the polo pony stallion Field Marshal, which stood in the Forest in 1918-19 and whose stock were then eligible for registration. Brookside Judy's line could be traced back to a Fell pony, from which she obviously inherited her exceptional bone. Another outstanding pony, bred by Miss Edith Jackson, was Brookside Olivia (by Newtown Spark ex Marcia), whose pedigree also includes Brookside Firelight, Brookside Shrimp, Field Marshal, and, in the sixth and seventh generations, the Welsh ponies Bahillion Bay Ruby and Bahillion Bay Lucy. Her Welsh ancestry was so apparent that when she was shown by the late Miss Hilary Kirkus, many people were convinced she was pure Welsh.

Other prominent names during the inter-war years were the Landers, the Brambles, the Doveys, the Andrews and the Burrys, most of which are still well known in the Forest today. None of these breeders, not even the Misses Jackson, ran studs in the modern meaning of the word, for most of their ponies ran out either on the Forest or on land in the district, such as Stanpit Marshes near Christchurch. The present-day practice of having separate stud farms with stallions in hand and visiting mares has developed within the last 30 years.

POST-WORLD WAR II STALLIONS

A group of stallions bred in the Forest during and immediately after World War II are now recognised as the foundation stallions of the post-war years, and the vast majority of present winners have one or more of these in their pedigrees. The stallions were Denny Danny, Goodenough, Broomy Slipon, Knightwood Spifire and Brookside David. They all died just a few years ago, aged well over twenty.

Denny Danny was a grey whose pedigree went straight back to the Dyoll Starlight Welsh ponies introduced by Lord Lucas. He was very Welsh in appearance, especially his head. He was small but with good flat bone, good shoulders, depth, and good action, though rather weak in the hocks and with a low-set tail, both of which characteristics he was inclined to pass on. He was owned and bred by Mr Hoyle, and won the Minstead Cup (the Championship) at Burley in 1951 and 1952. He was the foundation stallion of the Sibley's Merrie Stud.

Goodenough was foaled on the Forest in 1946. His sire was unknown but his dam, which belonged to E. F. Sparks of Sway, was a grey Welsh type, reputed to be a daughter of Field Marshal (and *his* dam was a black Welsh). She ran in Oakley inclosure and was known as The Ghost, from her habit of flitting through the trees. It is possible that when Goodenough was about fifteen, the mare was registered as Meadend Meadowsweet, in which case the stallion Burton Starlight was in-bred to her.

Goodenough also had the Welsh look, with fine legs and a bit of feather on the heels, and the typical Welsh stance. As a three-and four-year-old he was shown at the breed stallion show and won premiums. Then he was bought by F. C. Bennett and won the Bramble Memorial Trophy for the best five-year-old stallion in 1951. He won the breed championship three years in succession, after which he was taken off the Forest and stood at stud privately. He won one of the coveted special premiums at the Ponies of Britain stallion show for Best of All Breeds in 1956, but in that same year he unfortunately lost an eye in an accident, and his show career was ended. However, in 1957 he gained a Ponies of Britain special award for the stallion whose progeny won most points at the spring and summer shows. Unlike Denny Danny's, Goodenough's stock do grow well. Some of them are inclined to be a little light of bone and rather heavy topped and heavy necked, but they have great quality: Burton Starlight, for instance, is a classic example of all that is best in Goodenough's descendants. One of the minor foibles of Goodenough's stock is an inclination to chew things – one even contrived to eat a watch glass – but their Forest hardiness seems to preclude any ill effects.

Broomy Slipon has proved a very popular sire, chiefly because of his rich red chestnut colour and delightful temperament. His conformation probably did not quite match the other stallions, but he had more bone for his size than most. By Telegraph Rocketer out of Judy, and bred by the late H. J. Andrews, Slipon was a real Forest pony, running out for eighteen seasons. He was taken to Burley show in 1948, where he won the cup for the best foal, and after that he won many premiums, including his last at the age of twenty, when he stood sixth in his class. He was broken to ride and drive when he was rising four, taking it all in his stride as a good Forester should, and so perfect was his temperament that he could go for a year without being ridden and then do a good day's work without any trouble. His owner, R. T. Andrews, tells a remarkable story that illustrates the point. Mr Andrews was out colt-hunting on Stoney Cross Aerodrome after a wild bunch of mares; the pony he was riding had had enough, and he was wondering how he could keep going when he spied Slipon grazing with his mares. He jumped off his exhausted pony, caught the stallion, saddled him and drove the ponies into Fritham Pound. Slipon was then released, and returned happily to his mares.

Knightwood Spitfire, belonging to Mrs Pam Harvey-Richards, was probably the most striking of the quintet, being a dun with yellow eyes. He was by Brookside Spitfire out of The Weirs Topsy. (Topsy was herself by Clansman, a black Highland pony, and as far as can be established, almost every dun pony bred on the Forest has descended from him.) Knightwood Spitfire's strongest point was his excellent hind legs and well set tail, and he was a very good working hunter type of pony of about 13·2 hands.

Brookside David was the biggest of the foundation stallions, and although he tended to throw heavy-headed stock, he was much better behind than Denny Danny or Goodenough, and his foals invariably had good bodies and limbs, although a little inclined to be horsey rather than pony. He had one unattractive wall eye, which appeared in about 4 per cent of his stock. Some excellent ponies have come from crossing a Brookside David with a Goodenough or a Denny Danny – resulting in a better behind from the former and a better front from one of the latter.

Brookside David was by Brookside Firelight (with Field Marshal four generations back). In some respects Firelight might be regarded as the real foundation sire, but he grew over height and was gelded as a three-year-old, so that he sired only a few foals; but these did include David and another splendid stallion, Newtown Spark. David himself was hand-reared, and, although born on the Forest, never ran on it as a stallion. He was bred by Miss Jackson and Miss Golby, and his dam, Rhona, was sold just before he was born on the condition that Miss Golby would have the foal. To her astonishment the new owner turned up with the foal when it was only a few days old, saying that the mare had very little milk. So Miss Golby hand-reared David, and later sold him to Ted Burry, who ran him on Stanpit Marshes at Christchurch. Brookside David stock are in great demand both in Britain and overseas, as they have a wholly justified reputation for being exceptionally easy to handle and break.

Perusal of the pedigrees of the best ponies will almost invariably reveal the names of at least one of these five foundation stallions. For example, the three times breed society champion Oakley Jonathan was by Brookside David; and Jonathan's son Peveril Pickwick won eighteen championships in 1974 and started 1975 with a win at the Ponies of Britain stallion show. Denny Danny's distinguished descendants include Beacon Perdita and Beacon Pericles, and Goodenough sired some lovely ponies, such as Edithmay out of F. C. Bennett's exceptional brood mare, Setley Poppet.

PRIVATE STUDS

Since World War II, and particularly since the relaxation of the rules for stud book registration, which had made it impossible for ponies bred outside the Forest to qualify, many private studs have sprung up all over the country. They spread slowly at first, but increased rapidly with the boom in horse and pony breeding in the late 1960s and early 1970s. The modern definition of a New Forest pony for purposes of registration is as follows:

A pony is eligible for registration in Section A of the Stud Book if its sire is registered in the New Forest Stud Book or the New Forest section of the National Pony Stud Book and holds either a Ministry of Agriculture Licence or a Veterinary Certificate of freedom from hereditary unsoundness and if not running on the open Forest a return of all mares served has been received by the Hon. Sec. The dam must be a mare registered in the New Forest Stud Book, or its appendix, the New Forest section of the National Pony Society's Stud Book, or the Local Record. A mare or filly is eligible for the appendix if its sire is registered as above and its dam is known to the Registration Committee as being of pure New Forest stock running on the Forest. Provided in both cases the pony is neither piebald nor skewbald and does not exceed 14·2h. Colts whose dams are known to the Registration Committee as of pure New Forest stock as above will only be accepted as geldings.

THE BURRY PONIES

Of all the breeders in the post-war years, probably none did more to popularise the ponies at home and overseas than the late A. E. 'Ted' Burry. His Mudeford ponies are to be found in nearly every country where the New Forest breed is known. Mr Burry and his daughter Olive owned and bred really wonderful animals, notably Brookside David; and one of the most famous of all forest mares is Miss Burry's Dolly Grey IX. By Brookside Firelight out of Mr Burry's Mudeford Dolly, she was the result of one of those happy unplanned matings that occur from time to time with spectacular results. In the spring of 1941 the late Miss Edith Jackson won the two-year-old class at the stallion show with Brookside Firelight. He was big and well grown even then, and she did not want to turn him out on the Forest. Mr Burry said he could run at his farm with 'the old grey mare' Mudeford Dolly – and the result was Dolly Grey.

The mare had a phenomenal show career, winning fifty-one firsts at major shows from the time she was a yearling. Riding classes, in-hand, open or New Forest classes, she won them all, including the O. T. Price Challenge Cup as the Best in Breed at Burley no less than five times – as a yearling two-year-old, three-year-old, and twice as a brood mare. In between her show appearances this wonderful mare produced many winning foals. Her first, Grey Mist, was, like Dolly herself, bred by chance. In the winter of 1946 she was turned out on Mudeford marshes, where Brookside David saw her, succumbed to her charms, and jumped into her field. That summer at Burley show her admirers wondered why she was so sluggish and unlike her usual self. The reason became apparent ten days later, when Grey Mist arrived. Grey Mist herself won the Princess Margaret Trophy for the best New Forest pony at the National Pony Society Show at Roehampton. Among Dolly Grey's other distinguished other progeny were the stallion Dorian Gray and the mare Grey Magic, both by David Grey and both champions in their own right. At the age of fifteen Dolly Grey retired from the show ring. In an article about her in the annual report of 1956 the pony society secretary wished her many years of good grazing, and that wish has been answered: in 1975, at the age of thirty-four, Dolly is still as bright as a button as she grazes the marshes at Christchurch.

The Burry ponies have become a legend, as has 'Old Ted' Burry himself. A real pony man, with an encyclopaedic knowledge that he shared generously with anyone wise enough to listen, he was also a great character. It was he who virtually started the post-war export ball rolling, and a delightful story is told of his dealings with a group of foreign buyers. Old Ted and his customers were seated round his dining room table – and he had taken great care to place the whisky bottle firmly in front of his visitors, and the teapot under its cosy in front of himself. Communication was, to say the least, a bit difficult, but the whisky and a bit of shrewd showmanship worked wonders. The foreigners sat facing the fireplace, where prominently displayed on the mantelpiece was an impressive card saying 'Champion Male – Royal Show'. What the guests did not know was that at the Royal, colts could only compete as yearlings in a class that also included fillies. Consequently a colt could be placed only fifth or sixth in the class and still be named as Champion Male!

THE PRIORY PONIES

Another name which has been to the forefront of pony breeding for the last 20 years is that of Mrs Dennis Green with her Priory ponies. Mrs Green bought Priory Pippin in 1944 as a sucker at Beaulieu Road for 11½ guineas (surely one of the great sale bargains). Pippin was a genuine Forester, bred by the late F. Shutler, by a Forest horse out of Burley Bracken (who used to run at Burley). Pippin produced the massive number of twenty-two foals, won at Richmond when she was over twenty and even beat Dolly Grey in her younger days. Her first foal (by Brookside David) was Priory Bandbox, a champion in her own right whose grandson by Burton Sunlight is Priory Sunshade (Australia); her third foal, Sweet Sue II (also by David), was exported to Sweden, as was Priory Pandora; and her youngest was fifth at Windsor as a leading rein pony in 1974.

Pippin's most famous daughter, however, is the charming Priory Pink Petticoats (by Priory Gay Gordon), who, although successful as a two-year-old, really came into her own in 1965 as a three-year-old, when she was champion or reserve in every class she entered, including the Royal (champion), Ponies of Britain (champion) and National Pony Society, and followed this up by becoming champion riding pony at Burley, New Forest, Romsey, Royal Counties, Windsor and many others too numerous to mention. In 1967 she was supreme champion at Burley and unbeaten throughout the season. She is now a highly successful brood mare, having won the championship at Burley, and having become the first winner of the Whitbread Performance Pony of the Year award. 'Pinkie' has the most delightful temperament, which she appears to have handed on to her children – her 1975 foal is a beautiful colt by Burton Sunlight. Pinkie's son Priory Black Boots is an up-and-coming six-year-old with some fine wins already; he is a grandson of Mrs Green's exceptional stallion Priory Starlight (by Goodenough). Starlight's progeny and their descendants had, and are still having, a considerable impact on the breed. His daughter Peveril Pipette is the dam of Mr and Mrs Roberts's Peveril Pickwick and of Mrs Haycock's prolific winner,

Peveril Taylor Maid. At the stallion show and at Burley in 197.
the line-up consisted almost entirely of Starlight's sons and grand
sons.

Few people would deny that Starlight's most distinguishec
descendant of the present day is Peveril Pickwick, who goe:
back through his sire, Oakley Jonathan, to Brookside David
Mrs Roberts had always admired Oakley Jonathan, and when she
heard that Mrs Haycock had one of his sons for sale, she jumped a:
the chance of buying him. Pickwick was a big, rather leggy colt, anc
not until he was a two-year-old did he begin winning. Since then he
has become one of the biggest in-hand winners the New Fores:
breed has known, and in 1974, apart from his incredible eighteen
championships, he also qualified for the Lloyds Bank In-hand
Championship and took the Otton In-hand Pony of the Year
award.

Pickwick is a real 'character' pony (as so many Foresters are),
and, although exceptionally kind and gentle, he leaves no one
(animal or human) in any doubt that he expects certain standards
to be maintained! At a recent show, just as the New Forest class
had been lined up with Pickwick in his accustomed place at the
top, another stallion broke loose and created something of a
commotion. The other stallions in the line responded by leaping
about, but Pickwick stood in dignified silence, with a look of utter
disdain on his face, until the 'common herd' had quietened down.
At home, when led past boxes containing other stallions, he
puts on a great show, prancing along with an elevated 'parade'
trot; but, when they are out of sight, he relaxes and wanders
placidly into his paddock or stable. Uninvited and unwelcome
dogs in his paddock are dealt with quietly but effectively by the
simple means of fixing them with an imperious stare and advanc-
ing very slowly, one small step at a time, and with ears right forward – a method that has never failed. Mrs Roberts recalls that if
her children were asked to do a stable job they did not like, and
tried to enter Pickwick's box in a disagreeable mood, he made it
more than clear that he would not allow anyone in while they were
in that frame of mind. As a stallion he is used as a teaser to over
100 mares that come to his owners' TB and Cleveland Bay horses

each year, and this duty he performs with perfect temper. He adapts quickly to the temperaments of his own mares, and is kind and clever with the difficult ones.

Peveril Pickwick's sire, the great Oakley Jonathan, was owned and bred by Charlie Purse of Burley, and won the breed supreme championship at Burley three years in succession, thus equalling the record held by F. C. Bennett's Goodenough. Jonathan was taken off the Forest and shown as a yearling at the stallion show, where he was reserve for the yearling cup. He then took the two-three- and four-year-old cups in 1954, 1955 and 1956, before taking the supreme award in the following three years, in addition to winning the stallion class at the Ponies of Britain and the stallion and best of breed classes at the National Pony Society shows. Jonathan was broken to ride, and carried his owner hunting, as well as competing in the point-to-point. Jonathan's progeny have always been very much in demand, and many have been exported. His dam, Oakley Bridget, was bred by Messrs W. & G. Blomfield and bought by Mr Purse as a sucker in 1947. Although she did not possess really classic good looks herself, she produced a succession of fine foals, including Brown Sugar, Sabrina II (by David Gray), Oakley Ebeneezer, (by Goodenough), Oakley Coleen (by Brookside David), and many other winners.

BREEDING STUDS

The well known Beechwood Stud at Burley belongs to the Hon Mrs Rhys, who has owned and bred some fine ponies. Two of her mares who produced excellent winning foals (many by Oakley Jonathan) were Brown Fern (by Minstead Rufus) and Newtown Enterprise (out of Newtown Folly).

Without devoting an entire book to the subject, it is impossible to name all the leading breeders and ponies that have contributed to the success and popularity of the breed in recent years. But no record of New Forest ponies would be complete without mentioning Mr and Mrs Taylor's Tomatin Stud and their champion stallion Tomatin Golden Gorse, sire of the 1973 breed supreme champion, Tomatin Harebell; the Sibley's Merrie Stud, and stallion Merrie Mistral, whose progeny have been exported to many countries; Mrs Cave-Brown Cave's Conistone Stud in Yorkshire; and Mrs Haycock's outstanding Peveril ponies, such as Peveril Petrina and her daughter Peveril Pipette. Mrs Harvey-Richards has also owned and bred some fine ponies, including Knightwood Spitfire and Knightwood Palomino. W. T. J. Eastmond's Nigger Step of Bridgelea (by Merrie Minstrel ex Poppets) produced some splendid prize-winning stock before being exported to Germany, including Luckington Minstrel and the 1975 Golden Horseshoe gold award winner, Bridgelea Starlight. Mrs Roberts has retained several Nigger Step mares to put to Peveril Pickwick.

Miss Macnair's Beacon ponies have been mentioned elsewhere but her great brood mare, Bettesthorne Kate (by Brookside Spitfire ex Bettesthorne Jessica), merits special consideration. Bred by Lady Mills, Kate produced 11 foals between 1950 and 1962, nearly all of them winners: Beacon Pericles and Beacon Peridita (both by Denny Danny) were NPS winners before being exported to Denmark and the USA respectively; Beacon Touchstone (by Newtown Spark) went to Holland and was champion there after success at the NPS; and his full sister, Beacon Miranda, also an NPS winner, was exported to Denmark. Kate herself was foaled in 1947, and her dam, Bettesthorne Jessica, was a sister of the stallion Bettesthorne Caesar. She was a big winner, performing the remarkable feat of running on the Forest all the winter, and coming straight in to win show classes in the summer.

With the rise of so many private studs the face of breeding has altered markedly since the days when all ponies were bred on the Forest itself. The studs are able to produce a succession of animals up to the maximum permitted height of 14·2 hands, using big stallions of a better quality, which would probably not survive the harsh conditions of their native heaths. A certain amount of resentment exists among the commoners who feel that the studs have cornered the most profitable part of the market, making it more difficult for them to sell their smaller animals. Ponies much over 13 hands do not generally do well on the Forest, yet those very animals, from 13·2 upwards, dominate the market for riding ponies; and in the present state of high food costs and general inflation it is almost impossible to sell anything but an exceptional animal under 13·2 hands except at a loss. The commoner, therefore, is faced with having to take foals off the Forest and rear them on his holding (if he has enough land), where they will grow on average about a hand bigger than if left out. Even then, many will lack the quality to attract good prices. Colour, too, has a not inconsiderable effect on market values. Chestnuts and greys are much more in demand than bays or browns, but unfortunately it it appears that the pigment-deficient chestnuts and greys are the very ones that lose condition quickly if left out.

The stud ponies, of course, are not faced with any of these problems, and in reply to the commoners' criticisms it must be said that the big prize-winning stud-bred animals are the ones that have for the most part created the demand for New Forest ponies. In some cases the extra size is accompanied by less bone and substance and a more 'tied-in' action, but stud-bred ponies are easier to sell to both home and overseas markets. Many admirers of the breed, in addition to the commoners, are disturbed by this trend, fearing the eventual loss of the genuine pony type, and in many instances a stud-bred pony and a Forest-bred pony are two quite different animals. Genetically, of course, they are the same, but the trend away from the stocky short-legged hardy little animals that roamed the Forest for centuries persists, and may be accelerating. It is to be hoped that the commoners will accept the fact that their ponies have a future as the invaluable foundation stock of the breed, and that the private breeders will (as many leading ones certainly do) come back to the Forest as often as possible, thus ensuring the continuation of the characteristics of hardiness, good action, and excellent temperament for which the New Forest pony has such a wonderful reputation in the pony-breeding world.

ACKNOWLEDGEMENTS

This book could not have been written without the help of a number of people who have given generously of their time and knowledge, and I would like to record my deep appreciation of the following: Miss Dionis Macnair, for allowing me access to the records of the pony societies, for making available a great deal of information she has collected during her years as Secretary, and, not least, for reading the manuscript and making a number of helpful comments and criticisms; Agister Raymond Bennett, for sparing so much of his time to talk to me about the life of the ponies on the Forest; Mr and Mrs Hugh Pasmore, Mrs E. H. Parsons, Mrs R. H. Stembridge, Mrs R. Bennett, Mrs C. M. Green, Mrs B. A. Roberts, Miss F. Hardcastle, Miss Olga Golby, Miss Olive Burry, Mr Colin Tubbs of the Nature Conservancy Council, Mr Eric Young and Mr Harold Lidbury of the New Forest Commoners' Defence Association – all of whom have helped me considerably with facts and photographs. Veterinary advice was kindly given by a local veterinary surgeon who has kept Forest ponies for years, but who must, because of professional ethics, remain anonymous. My thanks go also to those who supplied me with information about the ponies overseas: Mrs J. G. Holbrook (Canada), Mrs Nita Appleton and Mr Max Barkla (Australia), and Mrs A. A. Wodschow (Denmark). Finally, I would like to thank my mother, who has helped and encouraged me throughout the writing of this book.

ACKNOWLEDGEMENTS

INDEX

Page references in italic type indicate illustrations